A STRAIGHTFORWARD GUIDE
TO

UNDERSTANDING MENTAL ILLNESS

MARIANNE RICHARDS

STRAIGHTFORWARD PUBLISHING
WWW.STRAIGHTFORWARDCO.CO.UK

Straightforward Publishing
38 Cromwell Road
London E17 9JN

A CIP record of this book is available within the British Library.

ISBN 1903909 0 15

Printed by Bookcraft Wiltshire

Cover design by Straightforward Graphics

Contents

Chapter

1   Introduction 6

2   Madness and Sanity are Difficult to Define 9
Defining sanity & madness
Illustration – Madness, Creativity or Eccentricity? Diagram 1
Illustration – Mental Illness – What is it Like? Diagram 2

3   The Mental Health Act 1983   19
An outline of some of the 'Sections'
Questions of Ethics

4   From Detection to Diagnosis   33
How mental disorders are detected
The process by which a person is taken for treatment
How a diagnosis is made
Undisclosed cases of mental illness

5   Medical and 'Talking Cures'   41
Including:
ECT
Drug therapies
Drug design and the 'drug trials' system
Categories of drugs on sale at the Pharmacy
Psychosurgery
The 'Talking Cures'
Illustration: The Human Brain – Diagram 3a
Illustration: 'Brain Chemistry' Diagram 3b
Illustration: A Clinical Trial (3 diagrams, 4a 4b 4c)
Illustration: Medications & Remedies Diagram 5
Illustration: Treatments Diagram 6

6   Therapists 68
Counsellors
Psychiatrists
Psychologists,
Psychotherapist
Mental Nurses
Rehabilitation Officers
Occupational Therapists
Hypnotherapists and Hypno-Psychotherapists
Illustration: Primary Care & CMHT's Diagram 7

7   Therapeutic Communities And Hospitals 115
Care in the Community
Asylums
Psychiatric Hospitals
Self Help Groups
Support Groups
Therapeutic communities
Illustration: Living in a therapeutic community Diagram 8

8   Medical Case Histories 124
Brief Psychotic disorder – "nervous breakdown"
Depressive Illness
Eating Disorders
Mania
Obsessive-Compulsive Disorder
Personality Disorders
Phobias
Schizophrenia
Illustration – Development of a Brief Psychosis Diagram 9
Illustration - Poem by a Depressed Person Diagram 10
Illustration –extract: Beck Depression Inventory Diagram 11
Illustration – The Mood Cycles Diagram 12
Illustration: Onset and Treatment of a Phobia Diagram 9e

9   Non-Medical Approaches to Mental Illness 165
Social interpretations of mental illness

Harmony of Mind, body, spirit
'Stages of life'
The benefits of a balanced personality
Illustration: Maintaining Psychological balance Diagram 13
Illustration: A holistic view Diagram 14

10   Alternative Remedies & Self Help   173

Complementary practitioners
Aromatherapy/Massage
Chiropractic/Osteopathy
Crystal Therapy
Reflexology
Spiritual pursuits
Yoga

11   Reading and Web sites   179

Includes books (mainly non-medical), website URLs

Glossary of terms   186

Index   190

Symbols Used In The Text

For ease of reference, I have used the following types of bullets
throughout the book:

♦	Causes
➢	Cures or remedies
•	Explanations
❑	Questions & quizzes
▪	symptoms

*"If a man write a book, let him set down only what he knows-
I have guesses enough of my own"*

Goethe

Chapter 1

An Introduction

Welcome to the revised second edition of this book, and my grateful thanks to those who have given me their kind comments and useful suggestions. Needless to say, I am delighted that there were sufficient sales to warrant this new edition. I hope my readers have learned in their own lives, that such negativity and personal criticism can be turned into strong driving forces to succeed.

I am pleased that the publisher has allowed me to extend the scope of the book, and to add in some new sections within the case histories and the therapists. I have also covered the White Paper proposals for the revision of the Mental Health Act, which looks promising.

The treatment of mental illness continues to be a 'Cinderella' as far as funding is concerned. There are for example many, many more counselling hours needed in the community; many excellent counsellors who need work; many GP's who would love to employ them; but at the end of the day, have no funds to pay them. Sometimes it does not take much to make a huge difference; that is what is so sad about the lack of funding.

It is my strong belief that, by demystifying some of the myths of mental illness, creating more tolerance, we can create a healthy and supportive environment for those who daily suffer from these terrible illnesses, and for their relatives, friends and carers. We might also become somewhat of a pressure group, encouraging greater Government expenditure in treatment and research, and for supporting carers within the community.

Although my premise is that mental illness resembles many of the experiences we all undergo during the course of our daily lives, I am by no means advocating that those with serious forms of illness should not be hospitalised. There are times when such people need to be taken aside from the community, for their own safety and sometimes for the safety of the public.

In keeping with my theme, I want to add that such exclusion from the general run of public life is generally beneficial for anyone who is undergoing a mental trauma, who needs to consider a problem, or to heal a psychological wound of any kind. "Retreat", "asylum", "solitude", "time out"; whatever you might call it, a period of aloneness is healing for the human psyche.

As in the first edition, for ease of reference, each of the early chapters will have:

- a list of contents at the beginning
- a summary of contents at the end

This book, for the new reader, is as jargon-free as possible, and can be either read in its entirety or use for 'dipping into' the various subjects.

I will always welcome positive suggestions from readers, corrections from professionals, and ideas for inclusion in future editions, via the publisher. If you enjoy reading my book, then please recommend it to others. If you have suggestions for other books, then I would likewise be interested in your comments.

Marianne Richards
January 2002

Dedication

To my mother
'Hoping you found peace of mind at the end'

To my brother
'It is never to late to overcome'

To myself
*With the knowledge that it is never too late
to learn to love oneself*

"There is pleasure sure in being mad, which none but madmen know"

Anon

"Love is a kind of madness"

Anon

Chapter 2

Madness & Sanity are Difficult to Define

Contents of this Chapter:
An exercise
- If you were a witness
- The witnesses

A further example
What does "sanity" depend upon
- a question of place
- a question of time
- a question of effect on other people
- a question of ability to survive

Some proposed definitions
Definitions – The Mental Health Act 1983
Mental illness affects many areas of a person's life
What is the difference between 'being mad' and 'suffering a mental illness'

I want to look in this chapter at the difficulties involved in making a diagnosis about mental states, and to raise questions you can ask yourself.

An Exercise

In a busy street you see a man, dressed in white robes, muttering and pointing at the sky. Some people are afraid. Some laugh and applaud, believing it is intentional entertainment. Others are puzzled and watch him for a while, then carry on with their shopping. A group of tourists treat it as part of their holiday experience.

The Police arrive and arrest the man, who resists – they handcuff him and bundle him into a car. He appears in court, charged with being a public nuisance and resisting arrest. Several witnesses appear in Court, either accusing or defending the man.

If you were a witness:

Imagine that the robed man is any of the following:
- ❑ a Bank Manager
- ❑ an actor
- ❑ someone celebrating a birthday
- ❑ mentally handicapped
- ❑ under 12 years of age
- ❑ a foreigner
- ❑ epileptic
- ❑ 'speaking in tongues' -a religious fervour
- ❑ under the influence of alcohol or drugs

Taking each of the above in turn, consider:
- ❑ would this man's behaviour be considered 'rational'
- ❑ would you consider him 'insane'
- ❑ would you have much sympathy for his predicament
- ❑ would it influence your view if he was wearing

The Witnesses

- Our first witness in Court is a member of the public, who says the man is dangerous and should be imprisoned.

- The second is a Psychiatrist, who diagnoses schizophrenia, and recommends that the man be detained in a secure hospital for treatment.

- The third is the leader of an Arts Group, who says the man belongs to a group of street actors.

The Magistrate is about to pronounce sentence when the leader of a local sect appears, bringing with him three other devotees also wearing robes. They say the man is one of them, and are angry that he has been maltreated. He is bound over to keep the peace and freed.

A Further example

You observe the following two men:

The first is wearing a dress, a wig and stockings. He is walking in the middle of the road, bearing a large stick, on top of which is a heavy piece of metal.

The second is wearing a red long tunic covered in gold braid, with a long blonde wig. He is rushing across the road, trying to catch papers which are fluttering about in the wind. He is pursued by two policemen.

Before looking at the bottom of the page *, what is your opinion about the mental state of these two?

As a footnote, I recently read of a young man who had been ejected from a supermarket by Security Guards, who assumed from his scruffy dress he was a beggar. This happened to the unfortunate young man on three occasions. In fact, he was a charity worker doing his legitimate shopping, and was eventually given an apology by the store management.

The dangers in all these cases of pre judgement speak for themselves.

* *The first man is a High Court Judge, heading a parade of dignitaries. The second is a University Chancellor at a graduation ceremony.*

Madness, Creativity or Eccentricity?

The following people all experience a 'vision'

Person 1: I saw a vision of a Saint in my living room

Person 2: I saw a Saint. I was 10 years old that day. She said "happy birthday!"

Person 3: I saw a Saint. She was disguised as a nun

Person 4: I saw a vision like a Saint. She was walking along, outside a Theatre. It was showing "Jesus Christ, Superstar"

Person 5: I had a vision of a Saint - I painted it

Person 6: I saw a vision of a Saint in a grotto.

See if you would agree with the observer below, about which description applies to each person:

MAD   SPIRITUAL

IMAGINATIVE

CREATIVE   NORMAL

ECCENTRIC

One particular observer thinks:	The observer concludes the person is:
Person 1: He must be mad. A Saint would not appear in an ordinary house	MAD
Person 2: Children should be imaginative	IMAGINATIVE
Person 3: He's a bit odd; why should a Saint be disguised as a nun?	ECCENTRIC
Person 4: I saw that musical too; one of the actresses did look like a Saint	NORMAL
Person 5: I saw that man's painting; he is a wonderful artist.	CREATIVE
Person 6: Bernadette of Lourdes did really see an image of St Mary	SPIRITUAL

What does "sanity" depend upon

A Question of place
The robed man happened to commit his act of 'insanity' in a public place. His actions therefore must be compared with what passes for 'normal' behaviour in a public place.

What is 'acceptable behaviour' at an arts festival or in a private home varies considerably. Can we therefore agree that, to a certain extent, a sane or insane act depends upon where it is committed, and for what reason.

A Question of Time
If the man continued to display this behaviour for several hours or days, it might increase the likelihood of his being diagnosed as insane. If the behaviour continued for a few minutes only, the diagnosis might be different. Perhaps, then, insanity depends upon the period of time over which the behaviour takes place.

A Question of Effect on Other People
Our friend appears to have provoked a series of very different reactions. Whilst some people experienced him as a benign character, he appears to have upset others. Perhaps the effect on other people has to do with a diagnosis of mental instability.

A Question of Ability to Survive
Given that this man suddenly appeared on the street at what point would it be considered as to whether or not he needed help?

Some proposed definitions

Using the examples I gave in my earlier scenario, a person with a mental illness could be defined as a person who displays the signs of one or more of the following:
- displays disturbing behaviour over a period of time

- creates an adverse reaction on other people
- appears to be incapable of looking after him/her self

By now, you might begin to understand the shifting sand of the ground we are treading upon. To be diagnosed as insane, even temporarily insane, is a serious act with wide reaching social, relationship, and employment consequences.

I would define a mental illness, as:

that state of the mind, which either permanently or temporarily disables a person from living their life to its full potential, regardless of other considerations, such as physical health.

Falling in love, being bereaved, getting very angry over a severe injustice, losing something very precious, can all trigger 'unbalanced' states of mind, which parallel some of the emotional states experienced by people undergoing a mental illness. In fact, a deeply emotional event (positive or negative) can trigger a permanent or temporary episode of insanity. Yet, these conditions are not tainted with the socially-financially-psychologically damaging label 'mental illness'.

Given a 'normal' or 'mentally ill' person, there are no actual physical difference to the brain. Mental illness is distinguished by internal chemical or electrical interruptions, faulty messaging systems. Hence, generally the lack of empathy which is a characteristic for those who have physical and therefore recognisable symptoms. Perhaps also it is because mental illnesses cannot be "seen", it therefore cannot be understood by members of the public.

Another simpler definition might therefore be:

- *someone who needs treatment for a condition which has altered the chemistry of the brain* or

- *someone who has suffered in their personal life, and suffering has triggered an unbalanced mental state*

There are people with severe mental illnesses who are dangerous, and have to be locked up for the safety of the public and for their own protection. Some are treatable, others are not. These cases become high profile by being reported in national newspapers. However, given how common mental illness is, and how many of us will suffer from one form or another during the course of our lives, the percentage of 'dangerous' people is very small. Even those with severe illnesses, such as schizophrenia, will go about their daily lives, even hold responsible jobs, with the correct treatments. No one will be aware of their problem.

Definitions – The Mental Health Act 1983

Even the Government finds it difficult to define exactly what is meant by mental illness. This is understandable, given that there are times when every one of us could be considered to be in an abnormal state of mind.

The new definition of mental illness, as outlined in the recent Government White Paper, is "any disability or disorder of mind or brain, whether permanent or temporary, which results in an impairment or disturbance of mental functioning".

Mental Illness Affects Many Areas of a Person's Life

Undergoing, or being diagnosed with, a mental illness will affect all the areas of a person's life, that is, it will have:

	that is:
psychological affects:	how you feel (your mood)
behavioural effects:	how you react to situations

15

| social & employment issues: | how you behave with others socially or at work |
| physical aspects: | how other people perceive your appearance |

The Difference Between 'Being Mad' and 'Suffering A Mental Illness'

'*Mad*' is an emotive term. It can have many meanings; a benign but 'mad' professor; a dangerous serial killer; a temporary insanity we call love. The term 'mad' is used in a wide range of situations to describe odd behaviour. It is not a medical term nor a diagnosis. 'Mad' implies lack of wholeness, out of control, lack of hope, fear, a permanent condition with no hope of a cure.

'Mental illness', is an illness of the mind; either permanent or temporary. It is a medical term, covering a wide range of diagnoses, from depressive illness to schizophrenia. An 'illness' is something which we would hope had a cure of some kind.

Given the two terms above- would you have more warmth towards someone whom you were told had 'a mental illness', or towards someone who was described as 'mad'?

Let us then dispense at once with 'madness'; from now on, we use the term 'illness'.

What is the Difference Between 'Mental Illness' and Stress?

Much later in this book, when you have read and digested the information, I will postulate that there is no difference between stress and mental illness; it is merely a degree of the severity of the problem.

Summary Of Chapter 2

What is Mental Illness? What is Madness? What is Sanity

An exercise
A gibbering man, clad only in a robe. Two men in strange costume, acting in what appears to be 'bizarre' ways. Trying to understand the signs of 'mental illness'

Does "sanity" depend upon any conditions?
- Place   where it is committed, and for what reason.
- Time   a particular time frame.
- Effect   the effect on other people

Ability to Survive
Some proposed definitions for mental illness:
- displays unusual and disturbing behaviour over a given period of time
- creates an adverse reaction on other people
- appears to be incapable of looking after themselves

Definition of mentally ill – The Mental Health Act 1983
'*Mental impairment*' and '*severe mental impairment*' are defined, but 'mental disorder' is not. Yet, the Act is based on regulations which deal with *the 'reception, care and treatment of mentally disordered people'*.

Mental illness has an effect upon many areas of a person's life
- psychological affects   how you feel (your mood)
- behavioural effects   how you react to situations
- social & employment issues   how you behave with others socially or at work
- physical aspects   how other people perceive your appearance

'Madness' implies a frightening, incurable condition. Mental illness' implies a condition which might be treated or cured (in a similar way to physical illness).

Mental Illness

What is it Like?
An Imagination Exercise

Look at the list on the left hand side of symptoms; then focus your attention on the "feeling" which goes with that symptom. Now try to imagine that feeling. To help you, I have listed under "imagine you are…" some ideas which might help you to imagine how it might be if YOU had that particular symptom.

Remember, someone with a mental illness might have more than 1 of the symptoms, and at the same time they have to cope with their daily lives. Imagine how difficult and painful that might be for them.

	feeling	imagine you are:	
DEPRESSED	isolation	alone; no friends, family, pets	) these are
	grief	bereaved, lost a precious thing	) all common
	shock	hear unexpected bad news	) feelings for
	exhausted	have totally exerted yourself	) someone who has
	self loathing	have deliberately hurt a friend	) depressive illness
HALLUCINATING	afraid	See something, but the person next to you does not see it, and does not believe you	
MANIC	'high'	hysterical- you cannot control yourself	
OBSESSED/ DELUDED	wanting	thinking constantly about something you want, but know you can never have	
PHOBIC	scared	imagine something you once mildly disliked, but has suddenly, for no reason, become a fearful thing	
PSYCHOTIC/ PARANOID	terrified	having a nightmare, but when you wake, the nightmare is still there	
	insecure	imagine that even people you love are trying to kill you, and there is no one to turn to	

'I am but mad nor' nor' west
When the wind is southerly, I know a hawk from a handsaw'
Hamlet, William Shakespeare

Chapter 3

The Mental Health Act 1983

The Contents of this Chapter:
Overview
Proposals for changes – the Government White Paper
Definitions of Staff Involved Within the 1983 Act:
The following Sections of the current act briefly outlined:

- ApplicationApplication for Admission
- Section 1   Definitions [*see Chapter 2*]
- Section 2   Admission for Assessment
- Section 3   Admission for Treatment
- Section 4   Emergency admission
- Section 20 Renewal of a Section
- Section 23 Discharge
- Section 57/ Treatment with Consent
- Section 62   Urgent Treatment
- Section 93 Management of Financial Affairs
- Section 134 Withholding of Correspondence
- Section 135 Power to Enter (Private) premises
- Section 136 Removal Public Places

Statistics

In chapter 3, I outlined how difficult it is to define 'madness', 'mental illness' and 'normal' behaviour in certain circumstances.

Society has to have a legislative way of dealing with mental illness, where it threatens the safety of the sufferer or the public. In the United Kingdom, this means takes the form of the Mental Health Act 1983. This Act was based on circumstances in the 1950's, where there was very little effective medication, and most treatment took place within secure hospitals. Very few mentally ill people were treated in the Community.

The Mental Health Act 1983 was set up by the Government to regulate the conditions of: "The Reception, care and treatment of mentally disordered patients, the management of their property and other related matters".

The Act itself is divided into Sections – areas or 'chapters' if you like. "Sectioning" is often used in a colloquial way, when referring to how a person is taken into care for mental health purposes.

Each Section covers a specific area, from first admission to Hospital for Assessment, to final discharge and aftercare.

Proposals for Changes in The Act

What I am about to describe is under scrutiny by the Government, who have produced both a Green Paper, inviting comment by both organisations and individuals; and a White Paper, outlining their proposals for the new Act. Both papers, and comment from Alan Milburn and Jack Straw, have been published in full on the Government web site. Mr Milburn, the Minister for Health, has commented publicly:

"For too many people care in the community has become 'couldn't care less in the community', sometimes with tragic consequences. I intend to change the law to give proper protection to the public and to patients".

Mr Milburn did stress the fact that the majority of mentally ill people posed no threat to society, but that these measures were designed to deal with those with dangerous homicidal potential, or who were likely to harm themselves.

I would like to give you a brief outline of some of the proposed change, followed by a brief outline of some of the individuals concerned with applying the Act, and then a summary of some of the Sections of the current Act.

The White Paper

The Government acknowledges that "current laws have failed properly to protect the public, patients or staff" (quoted from "Reforming the Mental Health Act"). Under present laws, patients can only be treated compulsorily whilst in hospital, and clinicians are therefore powerless to act where a patient/offender is in the Community and in need of psychiatric help, but resisting it.

The Government now intends to overhaul the outdated Mental Health Act, and replace it with one with far more stringent controls over persons in the Community who might be a danger either to themselves (suicidal) or others (homicidal).

Part I of the White Paper, which the Government has recently issued, concerns the new legal framework, within which those requiring treatment in the Community can be given it compulsorily. Park II of the paper concerns the strengthening of current laws, and the implementation of new Community care.

The White Paper includes the following general measures:
- proposed new legislation for the compulsory detention and treatment of the severely mentally ill
- a statutory requirement for mental health teams to produce care plans for mentally ill people 'at risk' in the community
- similar assessment and specialist treatment of offenders and prisoners who are mentally ill

There are specific measures planned to ensure that the public is protected:
- rights for victims of crime to know when someone with a mental health disorder is to be released
- cross disciplinary 'information sharing', on violent and sexual offenders, between agencies e.g. Housing Agencies, Courts, Police

- the power of Courts to detain defendants suspected of being mentally ill, for assessment and treatment

Those detained under the new Act will also be given 'human rights' benefits:

- free independent advocacy for those who will be compulsorily detained under the Act
- new Tribunals making independent decisions about compulsory treatment

Finally there are plans for massive expenditure, and the setting up of new Agencies:

- £300m extra funding for extra mental health treatment services
- £126m funding for specialist services dealing specifically with Dangerous Severely Personality Disordered (DSPD)
- a Commission for Mental Health, who will report back regularly on the effectiveness of the new Act
- provision of 24 hour, 7 day care for those who need it
- extra Community outreach teams
- 57 extra 'crisis teams', providing services for 5,000 more patients
- £2m a year for 3 years, for research and development of effective, evidence based, treatment for DSPD patients, for example Therapeutic Communities (refer to chapter 7)

All of these measures have been designed to fill the many treatment 'loopholes' which existed under the previous Act. The Care in the Community Act had obviously failed to work, because so little had been spent on aftercare. Many former patients drifted into a worse mental condition, or committed crimes, which lead to a large increase in the prison population.

The new White Paper promises much to redress the current situation, both in the Community and in prisons, whilst providing a far greater scope for individual monitoring and care.

Definitions of Professionals Within the 1983 Act

The Act specifies in great detail the exact responsibilities of each of the mental health workers involved. For those unfamiliar with The Act, I will briefly identify the major players.

'Approved Social Worker' (ASW)

A Qualified Social Worker, who has been approved to make applications under the Mental Health Act, for a person to be committed to hospital under the Act.

'Mental Health Review Tribunal' (MHRT)

Consists of professional and non professional members – i.e. members of the public, as well as Lawyers and Medical members. This Tribunal is appointed by the Lord Chancellor, and is a legal body. The membership of these Tribunals is soon to be reviewed.

'Nearest Relative'

A close relative of the patient, for example spouse, partner, parent. If this relative is a spouse, they must be married to the patient, or have been living with the patient for at least 6 months. In the case of gay partners, they must have been living together for at least 5 years to fall into one of the accepted categories. The person must be over 18 years. If no relative exists, then the Courts can appoint someone to 'act' in this capacity.

'Patient'

A person who is hospitalized, then becomes known as a "patient", for the period he/she is in hospital. The word generally has no long-term meaning.

'Responsible Medical Officer' (RMO)

The person who will be responsible for the medical care of the person in Hospital; usually the Psychiatrist treating the patient at the time.

Sections of the 1983 Mental Health Act

There are over 100 different 'Sections' within the Act. These 'Sections' are very powerful pieces of Legislation (law), in the sense that a person suspected of suffering mental illness may legally be detained for lengthy periods in Hospital, whilst being 'assessed' by a Psychiatrist.

As you read the terms of the Sections, try to imagine yourself or a close relative being 'sectioned'. Consider how vulnerable that person is. Consider the medical and legal people involved; they will be making decisions which could have serious negative consequences for that person's whole future. Consider how it feels to be 'imprisoned' against your will, and how angry or helpless that might make you feel.

Once in a Psychiatric Hospital, there is also the more subtle danger of 'institutionalisation', where very rapidly you might become used to being directed, given your meals, sitting around aimlessly, and generally having many of the everyday offices of life 'suspended. After several weeks or months, you might lose your ability or will to live outside the confines of the hospital.

Applications for Sections

'Applications' have to be made for all of the following sections. 'Application' refers to the formal application papers which are completed, legally allowing the person to be admitted to Hospital for treatment. Applications have to be made by:

- an Approved Social Worker, who has seen the person within the previous 14 days
- Qualified Doctors of Medicine/Psychiatry

Section 2 – Admission for Assessment

Used for:

- Persons not previously admitted to hospital
- Existing patients of mental health service

- On application from 2 medical recommendations
- detention for up to 28 days
- Grounds for sectioning– suffering a severe mental disorder, which needs hospital assessment AND it is in his/her safety or safety of the public

Two Doctors may detain a person for 28 days under this Section. This is a very long time for someone to be in a Psychiatric Hospital for the first time – can you imagine how anxiety provoking this might be? How would you cope with 28 days in such a place, in the presence of often severely mentally ill and long term patients? The staff will be used to bizarre behaviours but to someone newly ill, it can be a very frightening and isolating experience.

Section 3 – Admission for Treatment

- Application by 2 medical referees
- Can be admitted for up to 6 months
- Can be renewed for 6 months on first application, then a year on all subsequent
- Grounds- in the interests of the safety of the patient, or protection of the public

This Section is intended for persons who have been previously committed under a Section 2, and is intended to allow extra time for treatment to take place. It cannot be imposed if the patient's nearest relative objects, under the present Act. Would you, as a relative, consider you had enough experience (with public safety in mind) to oppose a decision made by a Mental Health professional? Under what grounds would you feel this possible?

Section 4 – Emergency admission

- Only used in cases of emergency
- Application by 1 medical referee
- Can be admitted for up to 72 hours (3 days)

- Grounds – severe mental illness; unsafe for the patient (or public) for him/her to be left at large

This Section requires only the agreement of 1 Medical Referee. Consider, that the Doctor might be very tired, might not know the person, and might have to make the decision about this Section in a hurry. Consider, the person about to be admitted might be of a different culture, might perhaps be a particularly 'normally' lively or aggressive character. Might this colour the Doctor's opinion of that person? Remember, these are decisions which will affect that person's future.

Section 20 – Renewal (of a Section)
This section is applied if:
- The renewal of an existing section; for 6 months (1st application), then 1 year periods thereafter
- The patient will either improve, or at least not deteriorate, if further treatment is given
- The renewal is for the safety of the patient or protection of the public
- Mental Health Managers have to review the patient

Mental Health Managers are the members of the Mental Health Trust Board, with varying degrees of experience in mental health matters. These renewals are for 6 months to one year, which is a very long time for someone to be detained in Hospital. Imagine, how that person might be affected by other patients. Asylums were designed to protect the mentally ill, yet they often damaged the prospects of that person from returning to a 'normal' life afterwards.

Section 23 – Discharge
- Used before the end of a Section, when it is considered the patient is fit to be discharged
- The Nearest Relative can request an early discharge

- Mental Health Review Tribunal can overrule discharge, if the patient is considered dangerous
- A patient can remain in Hospital voluntarily, even if discharged

The procedure for a patient to be discharged is lengthy, and involves a 'Tribunal'; a panel of experts and lay people, appointed by the Lord Chancellor to make this kind of decision. Relatives have some say, but can be overruled by the Medical Referee or the Tribunal.

Might the mental health workers be 'looking for' signs of illness; would misinterpretations of behaviour or speech be possible? Might the person be afraid to face the 'real' world again, and therefore have a vested interest in remaining 'sectioned'? Might relatives want to discharge ill patients for their own reasons?

Sections 57 Consent to Treatment
This Section is for Consent to treatment with Psycho (brain) surgery or hormonal implants
- for a patient who has given voluntary consent
- the treatment must either cure or alleviate the patient's condition
- 3 medical persons must confirm that the patient understands the nature of the treatment

Psycho surgery includes the infamous 'lobotomy' (now a very rare operation); cutting of specific areas of the brain, in order to modify behaviour. In the past, such surgery had devastating effects on the person's intellect and mood. I will discuss Psychosurgery in the Medical Treatments chapter of this book (chapter 5).

Does 'consent' mean that either Doctor or patient will be fully aware of the implications? What is the alternative, for the patient and perhaps the public, if the surgery is blocked?

Section 58 Consent to Treatment (with a second opinion)

This Section is for Consent to treatment by medication or ECT (Electro Convulsive Therapy), for patients who:

- understand what the treatment involves
- have not given permission for the treatment*
- who are not likely to understand the nature and duration of the treatment*

* In these cases, the Mental Health Act Commission appoints a 'Second Opinion Doctor', who ensures that treatment is necessary and beneficial, even if the patient refuses permission for this treatment.

I was once reliably informed, by a Consultant, that opinions are divided roughly half and half, regarding success or failure of this treatment. Medications do not always work, and there are side effects which can be severe – shaking, memory loss, 'tics'(involuntary spasms of the muscles, often facial), weight gain.

Section 93+ Management of Financial Affairs

The gist of these Sections are as follows:

- medical evidence of mental illness is a prerequisite of these Sections being applied
- a person can be appointed by a 'Court of Protection' with a 'Power of Attorney'*

* *i.e. they are given legal permission to manage the finances of any person with severe mental illness (not necessarily a patient)*

- where the patient is on benefits, the DSS will provide an appointee to fulfill the same task

In all cases, the persons appointed have to keep financial records and report to the Court as required. They are also required to 'act in the best interests of the patient'.

Imagine you are mentally ill, but there still may be many moments when you are 'sane'. During this time, you are aware that someone else is looking after your finances. Would that make you feel vulnerable? Would it be too easy, to then let someone else care for more of your life – i.e. to opt out or give up? To be mentally ill, even severely ill, does not mean that you are always unaware of what is going on around you.

Section 134 – Withholding of Correspondence from a patient in Mental Hospital
This Section includes:
- right to open and withhold patients' outgoing mail, if the addressee has indicated that they do not wish to receive mail from the patient
- ditto, if it is felt* that this mail will cause distress to the addressee
- right to withhold incoming mail* in the interests of patient or others' safety
  * *by the Mental Health Act Managers (MHAM)*

Strict records have to be kept regarding all withheld mail and its contents. Any mail addressed to MP's or legal advisers has to be delivered unless these persons have given written that such mail is not wanted. This ensures that the rights of the person in hospital to contact these public figures is generally retained.

The patient can appeal to the Mental Health Act Commission for restoration of delivery of mail in all cases, except where the addressee has written that they do not wish to receive such mail. These are very thorny issues, as you can imagine.

Manic patients might send frequent letters, may make outrageous sexual suggestions, or other personal remarks (which, in the throes of illness, they genuinely believe to be true). The recipient might be embarrassed, angry or inconvenienced.

In these circumstances, what is your opinion regarding the Royal Mail's duty to accept and deliver stamped mail, despite the recipient's objections? Would you want such mail?

Vetting incoming mail being stopped sounds totalitarian – but what if the patient, in their delusion, is seeking bomb making equipment or guns or knives. How would the contents be known? Do you consider, that the Royal Mail's responsibility to deliver all mail safely, outweighs all considerations? It is not easy to legislate, yet still retain human rights.

Section 135 – Power to Enter (Private) premises

- A Warrant has to be obtained by an Approved Social Worker (ASW) from a Justice of the Peace
- Police Officers can then enter the premises, by force if necessary
- A police officer, Approved Social Worker, and a doctor must be present
- The person inside can then be taken into 'a place of safety'
- The person can be kept for up to 72 hours (3 days)

The purpose of this Section is to deal with persons who are in private premises, and are believed to need urgent treatment for mental illness. Imagine you feel yourself to be in a safe place (your own home). Then you are taken from that safe place, perhaps with neighbours looking on, and driven away to a Psychiatric Hospital. You might not know what such a place is like, what to expect. Would that make you afraid of what was going to happen?

Families may have waited for a considerable time for a 'Section' to be made. Imagine the stress of living in the same house as someone who is behaving in a bizarre way, especially for lengthy periods.

Section 136 – Removal of People from Public Places

- A Police Officer may remove someone from a public area, for mental health assessment

- The person can be kept in the 'place of safety' for up to 72 hours (3 days)

This is a very controversial Section. Where multi-cultural Communities exist, each having very different social, spiritual and religious beliefs, there is plenty of room for misinterpretation of behaviour (consider our friend in a robe in Chapter 2). Police officers are not trained Mental Health workers, although some Health Authorities and Trusts might provide courses on major mental illness.

Statistics

The following are the numbers of persons admitted to Hospital under various sections of the Mental Health Act:

- 1996/97   23,186
- 1997/98   25,415
- 1998/99   27,100
- 1999/00   26,700

These figures do not include the many day and Community patients who see Doctors and Psychiatrists for more informal treatment, nor do they include the many undiagnosed cases. It remains to be seen if these figures will decrease with improving medications and earlier treatment.

Summary of this Chapter:

Overview
The Mental Health Act 1983; why it was drafted, and for what purpose.
The new White Paper for review of the current Act
Definitions of Staff Involved Within the Current Act:

The following Sections briefly outlined:
- Application for Admission
- Section 1* * as described in Section in Chapter2.
- Section 2   Admission for Assessment
- Section 3   Admission for Treatment
- Section 4   Emergency admission
- Section 20 Renewal of a Section
- Section 23 Discharge
- Section 57/8 Treatment with Consent
- Section 62   Urgent Treatment
- Section 93   Management of Financial Affairs
- Section 134 Witholding of Correspondence
- Section 135 Power to Enter (Private) premises
- Section 136 Removal Public Places
- Statistics

Chapter 4

From Detection to Diagnosis

This chapter includes:
How a Mental Illness is Detected
- who would be likely to recognise a problem had occurred
- how would someone recognise a problem had occurred?

How would the person be taken for treatment?
- the Community Mental Health Team

The Differences between a Physical and a Mental Illness
The Brain as Controller
How a Diagnosis is Made
- case history
- physical examination
- medical diagnosis
- the diagnostic manual

Undisclosed Cases of Mental Illnesses

I do not intend to alarm the reader, who might go away thinking that he/she is suffering from any or all of these conditions (this is the danger in delving into any book on medical matters!).

How Mental Illness is First Detected

Who would be likely to recognise a problem had occurred
The first people to notice a problem might be family, friends, or colleagues. They would be aware of the person's usual behaviour or moods. Employers might notice some differences in their employee's mood, or perhaps in a decreased ability to carry out jobs which formerly had presented the person with no problems.

How would someone recognise a problem had occurred?
Two of the keynotes of diagnosis are differences in the person's usual behaviour and moods. As to when they might notice the changes, then it could be days, months, or even years – there is no fixed time.

Two of the keynotes of diagnosis are differences in the person's usual behaviour and moods. As to when they might notice the changes, then it could be days, months, or even years – there is no fixed time.

Changes in mood or behaviour might be so slight as to either be tolerated or not noticed until these symptoms became very marked.

At home or work, the person might begin to find work, which formerly had been easy, impossible to carry out. Physical and psychological changes might be marked (greater tiredness, or vastly increased energy; withdrawing from society, or being outrageous); or they could quite small, and be mistaken for the normal day-to-day mood or energy changes we all experience, such as 'normal' anger, sadness and joy.

Mood and/or behaviour changes could be accounted for by normal life events such as death, falling in love, losing something or someone, or being given bad or good news. Sometimes, there are no particular outside circumstances which could account for the illness.

The problem could be temporary, or not very severe; for example, who would want to attend a psychiatric hospital as a result of normal anger or sadness? Usually, a person is not taken for treatment unless the symptoms are so severe that the person finds it difficult to enjoy or cope with their daily life.

How would the person be taken for treatment?

A person can:
- present themselves to their G.P. or a Psychiatric Hospital
- be taken by friends or family direct to a Psychiatric Hospital
- be detained under the Mental Health Act

The last case only applies if they are considered by a Social Worker and/or a Psychiatrist to be 'a danger to themselves or the Public'.

Under the current Mental Health Act, no one can be forcibly medicated whilst living in the community.

The Community Mental Health Team

Having reached his G.P., the person with the problem might either be treated directly by the G.P., or referred to a Community Mental Health Team, who will designate a mental health worker to visit, interview (take a 'case history') and make an initial diagnosis. The patient can be seen at home, in the Surgery, or in a consulting room within a Psychiatric Hospital. Where these Teams exist, it is not always a Psychiatrist who is given the job of diagnosis, although he is responsible overall for the clinical work of the Team. The G.P. retains overall clinical responsibility for his patient.

The worker assigned to the patient will report back to the Team on the initial findings and diagnosis. I have outlined some of the different kinds of work/therapy carried out by the various therapists in Chapter 6. Weekly, the Team meet to exchange patients reports, take on new referrals, and discharge patients. GPs receive reports on their patients either on discharge or on demand. How is a diagnosis made? We need to look firstly at the differences between a physical symptom and a mental symptom.

Differences Between a Physical and a Mental Diagnosis

My dictionary defines a 'diagnosis' as "identification of disease by investigation of symptoms and history; a formal statement of this". Where a physical illness exists, a General Practitioner might have many clues which would help him in his diagnosis.

If a patient has a painful leg, and has recently fallen whilst skiing, the GP might notice bruising and swelling and conclude "You, sir, have a suspected fracture".

The patient, duly grateful, would comply with the further investigations; an x-ray in a local hospital. Following this, he would accept the usual treatment of plaster cast, bed rest and physiotherapy. His relatives would be happy at the results, and visit the hospital in droves.

Matters are more difficult where the symptoms are no less real, but within the area of the brain, where they cannot be 'seen'. The G.P. cannot look at his patient and make the initial statement "You, sir, are mentally ill". The G.P. would be likely to be taken to Court for defamation, and the patient would not believe the initial diagnosis. The patient might resist being incarcerated in a Psychiatric Hospital, under the treatment of a Psychiatrist.

The patients relatives might feel his case had been mis-diagnosed, or that the patient was feigning illness. Even if the patient and his relatives were to accept that mental illness existed, then the subsequent treatments (medication, lengthy therapy, a stay in a psychiatric hospital, or even ECT), would be accepted reluctantly. Relatives might be embarrassed to visit. I have worked in my early days with patients whose relatives have deserted them, either because of shame or because they could not cope with the idea of mental instability.

The Brain as Controller

The brain is a delicate instrument, more so than the other organs and body parts. It is the central controller of thoughts, feelings and actions. It also controls the 'autonomous' nervous system; the automatic systems which function continuously without conscious effort; breathing, heart beat, etc.

The brain is an instrument which has continuous use throughout our lifetime, during both waking and sleeping. Small wonder then, given this continuous use, if it occasionally malfunctions.

A 'mental' illness originates in the mind, rather than a 'physical' illness, which originates in the body. A mental illness can consist of many different aspects, for example, mood changes, out-of-the-ordinary behaviour, or failure of reasoning (thinking). We examined a few aspects of these areas in chapter 2.

How a Diagnosis is Made

Please refer also to Chapter 6 of this book, where I describe the work of the specific Therapists. What follows is a Medical Diagnosis, as performed by Psychiatrists, or mental workers, or even directly by General Practitioners, although the latter usually refer their patients on to mental health specialists.

Case History

A professional (General Practitioner or Psychiatrist) will take what is called a 'Case History'. The professional will sit down with the patient, in a Consulting Room or sometimes the Patient's own home, and:

- allow the Patient to 'tell his/her story' i.e. the major events of their life
- ask the patient if they had negative or positive reactions to these events
- ask about the patient's family health, both physical and mental
- enquire if they have noticed any changes in their mood and behaviour
- how they are feeling now

These questions will enable the professional to establish (respectively):
- where the problems might have started
- how well the patient is able to deal with life
- if there is any history of similar illness in the family
- how long the illness has been affecting the patient
- how serious the problem is currently

Physical Examination

The professional might additionally make other tests, such as taking blood samples, giving psychological tests, making a physical examination, all of which will help to determine exactly what the illness might be.

Medical Diagnosis

Finally, the professional is ready to apply all that he has discovered in the course of his tests, and make a diagnosis i.e. an attempt to put a name to the illness, using the Diagnostic Manual (see below) as a guide. Once the illness has been named, it can be treated. Methods of treatment are looked at in chapter 6 of this book.

The Diagnostic Manual

One of the tools a professional might use to help make a diagnosis is a book called "Diagnostic and Statistics Manual (DSM), the current version being "DSM IV". This is a manual which lists all the different conditions (criteria) which need to be present, for a particular mental illness to be diagnosed.

You might look at it as a kind of servicing manual. DSM IV lets the Professional know what they need to look for, and gives a range of the severity of symptoms. The guidelines in this manual are very precise, and have been arrived at through many years of observation and research. Each mental condition is given a set of numbers and letters, allowing the professional to note down (using these 'keys') the exact diagnosis in a systematic way.

Although this Manual is useful, the professional will also have to apply knowledge gained through experience with similar patients, knowledge of medical illness, and general life experience. Cultural factors are also very important in making diagnoses (refer Chapter 2).

Undisclosed Cases of Mental Illness

Mental illnesses can only be diagnosed, if brought to the attention of a General Practitioner or Psychiatric professional. It may seem obvious, but there are probably millions of cases not disclosed for various reasons. Some examples might be:

- the family or friends might tolerate 'odd behaviour
- the family itself might be 'abnormal', therefore 'illness' is normal
- depressive illness might be seen as 'normal sadness'
- mania might be seen as extreme high spirits
- the person might be cared for within their own Society
- fear of social stigmatisation by the family concerned
- illness would not be noticed in a person living alone

Summary Of Diagnosis Section

Mental Illness is Detected
by family, friends, colleagues, or employers.
They might notice changes in mood or behaviour

How is the Person Taken for Treatment
- presenting themselves for treatment
- friends or family can refer them to a G.P.
- they can be detained under the Mental Health Act
- The Community Mental Health Team

Difference between a physical and a mental diagnosis
problems within the brain are far more difficult to detect

The brain as central controller
The brain is the central controller of all our thoughts and actions. Given this continuous use over many years, it is not surprising if it occasionally malfunctions.

How A Medical Diagnosis Is Made
- taking a case history
- a physical examination
- medical diagnosis
- the diagnostic manual

Undisclosed Cases of Mental Illness
Mental illnesses can only be diagnosed, if brought to the attention of a General Practitioner or Psychiatric professional. Sometimes people are cared for by their community; sometimes fear of 'stigma' makes families keep the mentally ill person at home.

CHAPTER 5

Medical And 'Talking' Cures

This Chapter includes:
Is a mental illness the result of brain chemistry imbalance
Electro Convulsive Therapy (ECT)
Drug Therapies
- Designing and Marketing New Drugs
- Categories of Drugs for Sale
Psychosurgery
Psychological/ Psychotherapy/ Counselling
The 'talking cures'

Heavenly powers were once the only treatment for mental illness. Nowadays, we have more effective treatments on offer. In this Section, I will endeavour to explain the workings some of the medical treatments on offer for mental illness:

- electro convulsive therapy (ECT)
- drug therapies (medications)
- psychosurgery
- psychological/ psychotherapy/ counselling;
     i.e. the so called 'talking cures'

Consider – is mental illness the result of:

- a 'chemical imbalance' in the brain of unknown origin
- chemical imbalance caused by the patient's environment
- combination of one affecting the other?
- genetic factors; that is, a family history of mental illness

Diet, drugs and alcohol are known to be contributory factors to mental illness. Other factors are:

41

- birthing problems
- genetic factors (genes passed by parents to siblings)
- accidental brain injury
- poverty, poor housing, severe life stress

There are no indications that social standing nor education have any bearing on whether a person might develop mental illness. There is an old but cynical saying, that 'poor people (with mental health problems) are considered 'mad'; rich people merely 'eccentric'. Mental illness knows no boundaries, and affects people of all socio-economic levels.

Many medical practitioners might feel that living conditions have a major influence in the onset of mental illnesses. Others (fewer, I suspect) feel that brain chemistry alone is the cause.

Holistic practitioners are taught that mind and body are inexorably linked, and that the illness or health of one will affect the illness or health of the other (see chapter 9).

One area of agreement, I am sure, would be that mental health is a vital part of human happiness.

The following are treatments which might be given by medical practitioners. I will cover other treatments in a later chapter.

Electro Convulsive Therapy (ECT)

Please refer to diagram 3A which will clarify the text.

Chemical Transmitters and 'Normal' Functioning

Within the brain, there are millions of cells. Each is joined by the action of 'chemical transmitters', which transmit (electrically 'fire') mood enhancing chemicals from one cell to another, so that every cell in the brain receives a certain quantity of the chemical.

The action of the chemicals cause a current to flow between the cells in the brain. If you see an EEG machine (electro-encephalographic), the readout will show the flow of electrical current through the brain.

If the brain is functioning correctly, each cell receives the proper proportion of chemicals, and this is passed on around all of the cells of the brain. The brain chemistry is 'balanced' between all cells. A person with such 'balanced' brain chemistry will be able to function physically, and experience a normal array of moods (happiness, sadness, peace etc.).

Imbalanced brain chemistry
Sometimes, for different reasons, the chemistry becomes 'imbalanced'; that is, some cells receive too much of the transmitter, and some receive none at all.

It might be useful at this stage to look at the diagrams which follow, and explain what is happening.

 **THE HUMAN BRAIN:**
how messages are transmitted

Diagram: 3a

Key:

 =   A 'neuro' or 'chemical' transmitter. There are millions of these in every human brain. Each of these carry 'messages' from one brain cell to another, in the form of chemicals. These messages are responsible for every activity in our body, e.g. our thoughts, actions, moods.

=   A brain 'nerve cell'. The human brain is made up of billions of these cells. The cells are chemically connected by the 'neuro transmitters'(see above). They do not have a physical connection.

NORMAL FUNCTION

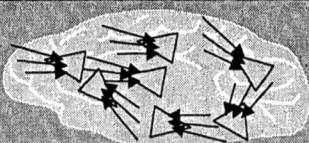

A functioning human brain, its millions of transmitters 'firing' normally. The transmitters and cells have no particular pattern; both this and the diagram below are simplified versions, for the purpose of explanation.

NORMAL FUNCTION

In this diagram, the chemical transmitters fire from one brain cell to the next in sequence. They 'jump' the gaps between the brain cells, just as electric sparks jump gaps. Each time, they take with them the chemicals which cause changes to the brain 'chemistry'. When the transmitters fail to 'jump the gap', the chemicals are not delivered properly to certain areas of the brain.

ABNORMAL FUNCTION

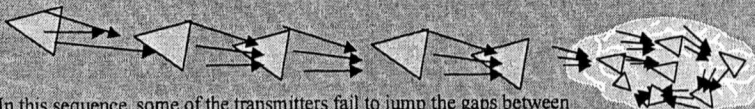

In this sequence, some of the transmitters fail to jump the gaps between brain cells, and do not deliver their chemical load.
The effect of this is sometimes referred to as: 'an imbalance in brain chemistry'
i.e. the chemicals are not 'balanced' between the brain cells, where they need to be.
On the right is another view of this event.

THE HUMAN BRAIN:
two methods of dealing with problems in 'brain chemistry'

Key:

= A 'neuro' or 'chemical' transmitter. There are millions of these in every human brain. Each of these carry 'messages' from one brain cell to another, in the form of chemicals and electrical impulses. These messages are responsible for every activity in our body, e.g. our thoughts, actions, moods

= A brain 'nerve cell'. The human brain is made up of billions of these cells. The cells are chemically connected by the 'neuro transmitters'(see above). They do not have a 'physical' connection; the chemicals and electric impulses sent signals from one cell to another

Electro Convulsive Therapy

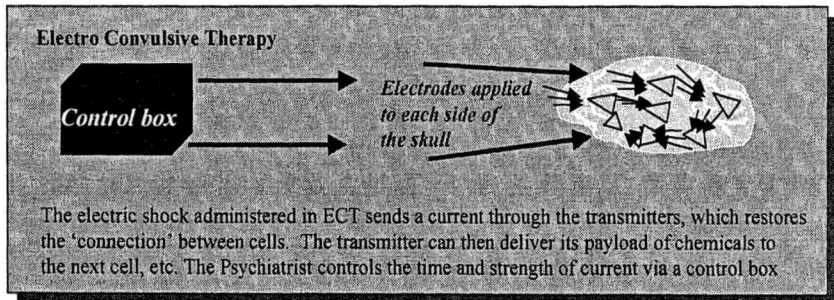

The electric shock administered in ECT sends a current through the transmitters, which restores the 'connection' between cells. The transmitter can then deliver its payload of chemicals to the next cell, etc. The Psychiatrist controls the time and strength of current via a control box

Drug Therapy

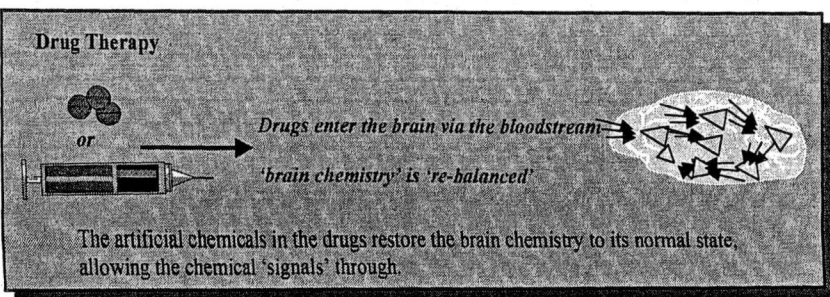

The artificial chemicals in the drugs restore the brain chemistry to its normal state, allowing the chemical 'signals' through.

When 'chemical transmitters' fail to work, the result can be marked mood changes. These are reversible once the chemistry returns to normal (the equivalent of repairing the wires in an electric cable). The longer the damage is left without treatment, the more difficult the 'repairs' will be, as the chemicals 'build up' in the brain.

Delivery of Electro Convulsive Therapy

A general anaesthetic and a muscle relaxant are given to the patient. This stops severe convulsions and any physical injury to the body during treatment. Electrodes (wires, attached to pads, which are placed on either side of the skull) deliver the electric current to the brain. The shock causes a convulsion in the patient's muscles. It is very like an artificially stimulated epileptic fit. A course of around 12 sessions is considered an average course of treatment. This treatment is generally used as a last resort, to relieve the symptoms of a chronic depressive illness. Not even medical people would be able to describe how this therapy works, and it is controversial enough that many might feel that it is not beneficial.

New Developments in ECT

Some very severe depressive illness has been successfully treated with ECT. The new version of this treatment apparently gives the shock to only one side of the brain, at lower voltages than previously, and is said to make the ECT more effective.

Drug Therapies

What are 'Drugs'

'Drugs' are chemicals, which have been designed by Pharmaceutical companies to treat specific illnesses, and are prescribed by General Practitioners, Consultants and Psychiatrists. They are referred to as 'medications'.

Anti depressant drugs are designed to assist the brain nerve cells to deliver their payload of mood changing chemicals to the right areas of the brain.

The term 'drug' is often used colloquially to describe the illegal use of these substances. Drugs such as morphine, heroin, cocaine, only become illegal when they are purchased or used or supplied by persons who are not qualified to prescribe or be prescribed to. All these drugs are currently used legally within the medical profession.

Drugs can be both curative and harmful. Sometimes, even the medical profession get it wrong, and prescribe either the wrong dose or a drug which reacts adversely with another drug.

Designing and Marketing New Drugs

New types of drugs appear on the medical market all the time. You may have noticed that, if you are on a particular 'brand' of medication for a long time, sometimes your General Practitioner will prescribe a different one. The Pharmaceutical industry and their scientists are always seeking to improve the quality of their product, as they learn more about how the human body and mind work. There are huge costs involved in the design and trial of new drugs.

New Drug Trials

Refer to the diagram within this chapter for an outline of how a trial is conducted. It is very difficult to give a summary of a particular trial, as the procedures are laid down individually for each new drug.

TIME
LINE

PROCESS OF A CLINICAL TRIAL ON A NEW DRUG: 1 of 3

NOTES

up to
15 years
in all -
perhaps
more

A new molecule is synthesised in the Pharmaceutical company's laboratory

If the chemical is to be produced on a large scale, they must design this early on; this will form part of the formal 'drug trial'

the disease the drug is designed to 'cure' is introduced into an animal (usually dogs or rats)

Company decide on exactly what the trial is going to measure, the quantity, and how long it will take

New drug tested on above animals, for beneficial and adverse effects

**PRELIMINARY STAGES -
initial discovery of a new drug
and animal testing**

Careful records must be kept at all stages, for the regulatory authority. If anything is wrong with the application presented, the company could have their application rejected, and trials will have to be closed

The drug is produced in quantity at one of the chemical plants of the drug company, ready for the first testing

Ethical questions surrounding the drug are taken into consideration at this stage

Documentation on the new drug is prepared by the Pharmaceutical Company for the regulatory authority

PROCESS OF A CLINICAL TRIAL ON A NEW DRUG: 2 of 3

<u>TIME</u>
<u>LINE</u>

<u>NOTES</u>

documents
prepared
from
day one;
includes
all details

| Pharmaceutical company propose to market the new drug | Developments made within drug company |

| Documentation prepared - covering every detail - e.g. drug characteristics, tests and results, adverse and positive effects on patients, manufacture methods, chemistry | Detail is recorded in a set format, which depends on the type of drug. Each 'trial' will be slightly different, but must adhere exactly to the regulations |

PHASE 1 OF TRIAL - testing for drug toleration

3 - 6 months

| 1 dose of new drug given to **healthy** volunteers | tests carried out in clinical environment e.g. special unit within drug company First volunteers are healthy individuals |

| 20 - 100 volunteers (drug company employees tested) | Very toxic drugs e.g. anti cancer, are only tested on patients, not healthy volunteers |

only about 7 in 10 drugs pass this first phase

PHASE 2- testing on humans

6 months
to
2 years,
possibly more

| * G.P. patients, who have the **relevant** illness/disease to the drug, are asked if they will take part in trials of the new drug. Aim is to see if it is effective in use | * many 100's tested, and any adverse effects, successes, side effects etc. monitored by G.P.s. |
| | This part of the testing may take years |

To make sure psychological factors do not play a part in the testing (e.g. patient and G.P. are anxious the drug should work, so they are keen to see only the positive side of the test) the drug company administer a 'placebo' (or non acting substance) to some of the patients. This is called a 'blind' test.

**TIME
LINE**

PROCESS OF A CLINICAL TRIAL ON A NEW DRUG: 3 of 3

EVENT   NOTES

up to
5 years
in all -
perhaps
more

PHASE 3 - large scale testing on humans

major clinical testing on a wide
range of G.P. patients,
- several thousand involved

Company can apply to the drug Licensing
authority to market the drug

NB no drug can be marketed
and sold in the UK, without
undergoing all these procedures
   This stage often involves
testing internationally.
   Large numbers of patients in
the trial are vital, if it is to be
successful

PHASE 4 - human testing after Licensing

When the drug has been used by
1000's of patients, some adverse
reactions might show up - if they
are rare, they will not show until
a drug has been on the market for
some time
e.g. lack of response to a drug, its
dosage, interaction with other
drugs, alternative ways of
administering the drug

limitless

Reports on the effectiveness of drugs after
they have entered the market are made by
doctors, pharmacists, hospitals, coroners

Thalidomide is one drug which was
withdrawn from sale, after horrific
effects were noted on children

If there are major problems with the drug at this
stage, it can be withdrawn from sale

General Stages of a Drug Trial

Preliminary Stages – initial discovery and animal testing
Every pharmaceutical company has laboratories, where chemists synthesize new drug molecules. Molecules are the small particles from which all materials are made; from a brick to a glass of beer.

Careful documentation has to be kept at every stage, otherwise the Company will not be able to legally continue trials for their new drug.

Testing is initially carried out on laboratory animals, usually rats and dogs. Tests are designed to discover both beneficial and negative effects of the new drug on the diseases it has been designed to alleviate. The disease is introduced into the animal, and all the effects of the new drug carefully noted. Not all drugs are tested on animals.

The scientists are particularly looking for signs of 'toxicity' (i.e. whether or not is it harmful) and 'mutagenicity' (whether it directly alters any of the structure of the organism).

Phase 1 Testing – on volunteers
After the animal testing stage, a trial drug is given to healthy human volunteers. Initially, volunteers are chosen from Pharmaceutical Company employees. Later, outside volunteers are called in. Payment is good for those taking part in trials. All tests take place within the Company's testing centre (if you are interested in being a volunteer, you can apply direct to the Pharmaceutical companies).

Very toxic drugs, such as those designed for treating cancers, are tested only on patients (i.e. those who already have the disease) rather than volunteers. There are very strict guidelines laid down for testing.

These trials are designed to discover:
- how 'toxic' the drug is i.e. how well the body tolerates it

- how the body disposes of the drug
- comparative responses on 'blind trials' *

* 'blind' or 'placebo' tests, are where harmless and neutral substances are given to certain volunteers, to compare their response that of volunteers who have actually been given the drug.

Phase 2 Testing – on patients

At phase 2, patients who actually have the disease relevant to the drug being tested are given the new drug. Tests will show not only if the drugs are effective, but also the dosages at which they will work, and what the 'negative effects' might be. Every drug will have some of the latter, as it is virtually impossible to separate only the positive benefits when a particular combination of chemicals is used to create a new drug.

When tests have been concluded, and large-scale trials carried out on actual patients, these ' negative effects' will appear in the General Practitioners drugs manual (MIMs) as 'side effects'.

All side effects have to be publicised, even if only occur in a minority of cases. They might range from headaches, to nausea, to stomach pains.

Phase 3 – large scale testing on human patients

This is a very important part of the drug trial procedure, and will determine whether or not the new drug is allowed a licence, without which it cannot be sold.

A large number of G.P. patients are asked for their consent to take part in the trials, and are monitored for their reactions to the drug.

The purpose of this part of the trial, is to demonstrate that the new drug is more effective, or of less risk, than drugs currently on the market.

International trials may be conducted, to gather as wide a range of data as possible.

Once this testing has been satisfactorily conducted (which may take up to 10 years), then a license to market the drug commercially will be granted by the Government. No drug can be sold without this license.

Phase 4 – testing after the granting of a license

Once the license has been granted, the testing is not yet completed. The Company will conduct Phase 4 tests, which will show up any difficulties in long-term use of the drug. Such problems may include:

- adverse reactions in long term use
- any negative effects when other drugs are used at the same time
- revised dosage or administration of the drug
- looking at cases where it is not effective, and establishing why

Animal Testing

There has been much in the press about the conducting of trials on animals. In some cases, the drugs companies are able to conduct testing on tissue culture, and avoid some of the research on animals. It is questionable whether or not animal testing can ever be entirely avoided. Perhaps should question, do we want to cure virulent and sometimes painful human disease and illness or do we not, and at what cost.

'Virtual trials'

Following on from the above subject, I came across a small piece whilst researching on the Web, which mentioned a new software package being used by Glaxo Wellcome (one of the largest pharmaceutical companies, based in the UK).

The software can be manipulated to simulate the behaviour of individual drug molecules. This will help cut out certain early stages of the drug trial process, but whether it will have an impact on the more sophisticated testing on animal tissue I am unaware. Those who have seen the recent BBC computer aided documentaries on dinosaurs, will be in no doubt as to the latent powers of computer programmers in the world of science.

The URL, for anyone interested is:
www.tagish.co.uk/ethosub/lit6/75ee/htm.

Categories of Drugs for Sale

You may wonder why, when you ask in a Chemist's shop for a certain medicine, that the shop assistant will either say that it is 'prescription only', or that it cannot be dispensed unless a qualified chemist is present.

The Medicines Act 1968, lays down guidelines about exactly which medicines can or cannot be sold 'over the counter' in this country. There are four classes:

- POM – prescription only; can be sold only on prescription
- GSL – general sale list sold over-the-counter
- P – pharmacy can only be sold if the pharmacist is present
- CDPOM (controlled drug prescription only) dangerous drugs ie very stringent   guidelines, e.g. prescription must be in GPs handwriting

Groups of drug types

Diagram 5 is an attempt to simplify the main types of medications, which act upon the nervous system. Although this is the 'medical therapy' part of the book, you will note that I have introduced in this diagram some of the plants which are used in holistic therapies, which help to alleviate the same symptoms. It is important to remember, that plants, roots, bark, and berries were in use as medicines for thousands of years before the giant pharmaceutical industries came into existence.

Many modern drugs are still made directly from plant materials rather than laboratory grown chemicals.

The following plants are examples of the originals of many useful remedies:

> curare – South American poisonous herb, used as a muscle relaxant in surgery
> belladonna (deadly nightshade) – to dilate eye pupils in operations
> digitalis (foxglove) – to regulate heart beats
> amaryllis belladonna (Belladonna Lily) –relief of Alzheimer's disease
> valeriana officinalis (valerian) – a sedative
> myrrhis odorata (sweet cicely) – anti-cancer research trial component
> mentha spicata (spearmint) – calming nervous disorders
> envallaria majatis (lily of the valley) – antispasmodic, and diuretic
> salix purpurea (purple osier) – the bark is the origin of aspirin
> asarum canadense (wild ginger) – used for head colds
> tanacetum parthenium (feverfew) – used for migraine relief

Wandering through the Botanic Gardens at Oxford in search of this information, I was struck by the beauty of some of these plants. Some of them have been used for many thousands of years as natural curatives, especially by the Chinese.

MEDICATIONS AND REMEDIES
drugs, plants, and foods

CHAMOMILE

VALERIAN

Diazapam

SEDATIVES
*'depress' the nervous system
and therefore diminish anxiety
also reduce paranoia, aggression,*

Librium

Alcohol

barbiturates
beta blockers
hypnotics
tranquillisers

Valium

Secobarbital

To treat:
anxiety
convulsions
insomnia
muscle relaxation

Largactil

ANTI PSYCHOTICS -
(major tranquillisers)
*reduce 'psychotic' symptoms
e.g. hallucinations
both visual & auditory*

Clozaril

Serdolect

Melleril

To treat.
psychoses
hallucinations
mania
schizophrenia

MEADOWSWEET

SAGE

ANTI DEPRESSANTS
(a form of tranquilliser)
*improves mood
relieves emotional pain*

Seroxat

Gamanlil

Prozac

To treat:
depressive illness

Distalgesic

Tylenol

ANALGESICS
*decrease
physical pain*

MARIGOLD

COMFREY

aspirin

To treat.
headaches
physical pain

CINNAMON

STIMULANTS
*stimulate nervous system
e.g. increase wakefulness,
loss of appetite*

To treat
psychoses
hallucinations
schizophrenia
tiredness

amphetamines
caffeine

coffee

FENNEL

The small boxes around the edge of
each hexagon are examples of brand
names of the drug types.

I have included the following for
interest:
bold type - drugs (chemicals)
bold italic - foods/beverages
SMALL CAPS - plants

There are 3 main groupings of drugs which act upon the nervous system:

> sedatives – which 'sedate' the nervous system.
> analgesics – which act as pain killers
> stimulants – which 'stimulate' the nervous system

We'll consider the sedatives group, which include many of the drugs used in psychiatric medicine. The sedatives are the major players, as far as mental illness is concerned, consisting of two major types; anti depressants and anti psychotics.

Anti depressants are designed to counteract the symptoms of depressive illness – including mood control, relief of emotional pain, promoting sleep. Anti psychotics are designed to reduce the symptoms of a psychosis; to reduce hallucinations, and control the mood.

Some Common Types Of Antidepressants

Antidepressants are drugs which relieve the symptoms of depressive illness. I use the word 'relieve', because they do just that; they do not cure the illness. Depressive illness is complex, and needs additional assistance, such as psychological therapy, and the patient's co-operation with therapy.

There are different kinds of antidepressants, which work in different ways. The three main types are:

- Tricyclics
- SSRI's (Specific Serotonin Re-Uptake Inhibitors)
- MAOI's (monoamine oxidase inhibitors)

For this section, it will be useful if you referred to diagram 5 which I hope will clarify what is a complex area.

Tricyclics

Two of the transmitters we discussed earlier in the chapter, which are known mood enhancers, are serotonin and noradrenaline.

As the name suggests, 'transmitters' transmit or deliver mood-changing chemicals between cells in the brain. In the case of a human brain, if the enough of the correct chemicals is not delivered, then the result will be a lowering of the mood, which we refer to as a 'depressive illness'.

Tricyclic antidepressants are drugs which have been designed to increase the number of natural chemical transmitters, which makes them powerful enough to jump the gaps between cells. This is like putting the correct voltage across an electrical circuit; your appliance will now do what it should, whether it is heating water or powering a drill; or in the case of a human brain, it will allow its owner to experience a normal range of moods.

Medication has to be taken over many months, perhaps years, in order to build up the number of natural chemicals in the brain, so that it will work without need of drugs. 'Tricyclic' refers to the ring like chemical structure of the drug. Examples of tricyclic anti depressants: Elavil, Endep.

SSRI's (Specific Serotonin Re-Uptake Inhibitors)
Serotonin is one of the chemical transmitters, which causes mood changes in the brain. This drug, like the one above, is designed to increase the amount of serotonin in the brain chemistry. Examples of SSRI's: prozac, fluvoxamine, faverin.

MAOI's (monoamine oxidase inhibitors)
The amount of monamines in the body controls the fluctuation of mood. MAO inhibitors are designed to prevent a build up of

monamines, and thus ensure that mood levels are stable. Example of an MAOI: marplan

Side Effects

Many of the drugs have 'side effects'. You remember during the section on drug trials, that I mentioned animal and human testing. Drugs are tested for effectiveness, safety, negative effects and cost effective manufacturing.

Chemicals in drugs are complex, and it is practically impossible to eliminate all the negative aspects of them in the human body. For example, some anti depressants may relieve depression, but also may leave the patient with effects such as headaches or drowsiness. Some anti psychotic medicines may leave patients, after many years use, with permanent shaking or twitching. Some medications may be dangerous when taken with certain foods ('contra indicative'), common foods being chocolate and cheese.

Patients can be prescribed drugs but, unless they have been detained under certain Sections of the Mental Health Act, are not forced to take them. If patients break off their treatment too early, the drugs do not have time to be properly effective, and symptoms return.

There are two more weapons in the psychiatric armoury against mental illness; psychosurgery, and the 'talking cures'.

Psychosurgery

Psychosurgery is surgery carried out on the brain. These are very serious operations, and only carried out where there is no other option. The brain remains an elusive area, and surgeons working on this area are highly skilled; there is no room for error.

Early Days – 'Trepanning'

The first examples of surgery carried out on the brain are up to 40,000 years old. 'Trepanning', or cutting a circular hole in the skull, presumably to let out evil spirits, appears to have been widespread in the Stone Age, Ancient Greece and Rome, and among many other cultures. Many skulls have been found with such holes in them. What is more surprising is that, according to the evidence of bone growth around the holes, many of these early patients survived these crude operations.

In the case of war wounds received to the head, or any kind of pressure against the brain, trepanning was (and continues to be) used as a treatment to relieve that pressure where there is a leakage of blood into the brain. For those of strong constitution, I have included some url's of websites which give some interesting information on the subject in chapter 11.

Phineas Gage and the Discovery of the Frontal Lobes

Among the most interesting of early cases is that of Phineas Gage, a railroad worker who accidentally drove a 25mm steel rod through his cheekbone and up through his skull brain, whilst exploding dynamite.

Immediately after this horrific accident, Gage became unconscious and had epileptic fits, but later recovered and lived for many years. Unfortunately, he underwent a personality change after his accident, and became very aggressive. He survived some 11 years after the accident, and much was learned from the study of his skull after his death.

Pre Frontal Leucotomy Operations

Surgeons studying Gage's skull were able to make conclusions about which areas of the brain were responsible for personality and mood. The rather dubious operation known as a 'leucotomy', where the frontal lobes of the brain were removed, was one of the results of this research. Leucotomies were performed on people with schizophrenia or problems of mood ('affective disorders'), but the results were variable.

I remember one lady from my volunteer days in an old Asylum in Scotland who had undergone this operation in the 1950's. The Ward Sister told me that the lady had been 'an intelligent young woman'. When I knew her, she presented as a sad child-like person, who wept a great deal, and was obviously not the lively and intelligent personality referred to in her early notes.

Psychosurgery was controversial from the beginning even among Psychiatrists, who felt that to interfere with personality through surgical methods was unethical.

TYPICAL TREATMENTS for
MENTAL HEALTH PROBLEMS
of varying degrees

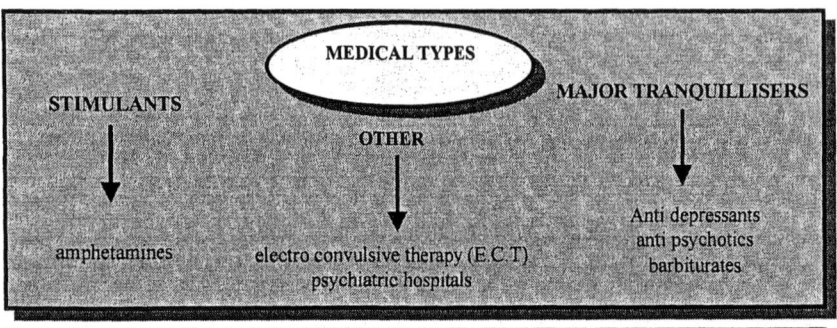

MEDICAL TYPES

STIMULANTS   **MAJOR TRANQUILLISERS**

OTHER

                                                      Anti depressants
                                                      anti psychotics
                                                      barbiturates

amphetamines   electro convulsive therapy (E.C.T.)
                       psychiatric hospitals

REICHIAN THERAPY

THERAPEUTIC   **PHYSICAL THERAPIES**
COMMUNITIES
                       OTHER TREATMENTS -
                            non medical

SELF HELP   **MEDITATION**

ARTS THERAPIES   **HOLISTIC THERAPIES**   **SUPPORT GROUPS**

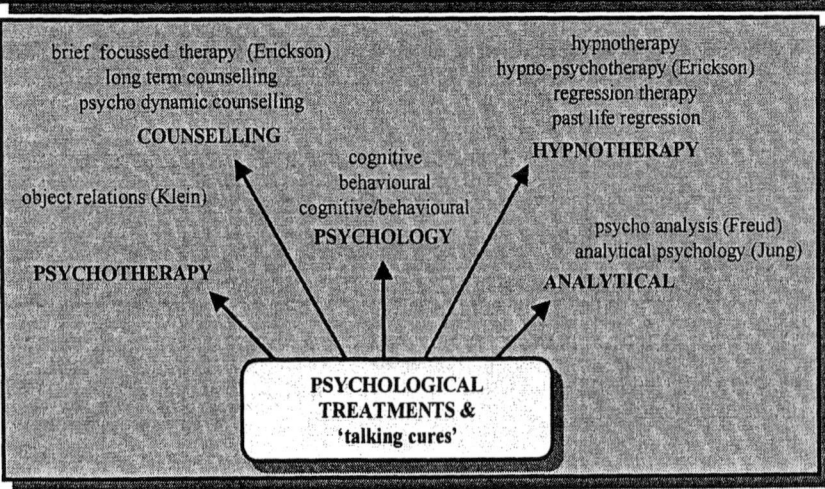

brief focussed therapy (Erickson)   hypnotherapy
long term counselling   hypno-psychotherapy (Erickson)
psycho dynamic counselling   regression therapy
                                                     past life regression
COUNSELLING   **HYPNOTHERAPY**

                                cognitive
                               behavioural
object relations (Klein)   cognitive/behavioural
                            PSYCHOLOGY   psycho analysis (Freud)
                                                     analytical psychology (Jung)
PSYCHOTHERAPY   **ANALYTICAL**

                        PSYCHOLOGICAL
                         TREATMENTS &
                         'talking cures'

The 'Talking Cures'

Successful 'talking cures', literally talking to the person about their life, their sorrows and their suffering, have proved that treatment without medications can be very effective. It depends upon the person involved, and upon the severity and nature of their illness.

The four major players in this treatment area, and responsible for spawning a huge variety of different 'Psychotherapies' were Jean Martin Charcot, Joseph Breuer, Carl Jung and Sigmund Freud. All of the modern psychotherapies stemmed from the pioneering work of these four great men.

Hypnosis

Jean Martin Charcot worked extensively with patients who were diagnosed with 'hysterical paralyses' of limb or voice, which are now referred to as 'conversion disorders' (i.e. the paralyses occurred as a result of traumatic psychological incidents, which became 'converted' to physical ailments).

Charcot discovered, that by using the deep form of relaxation known as hypnosis, he was able to use hypnotic suggestion to free his patients from their physical symptoms.

Following on from this, Breuer allowed his patients to talk under hypnosis, and discovered that this freed them from their symptoms. The term 'talking cure' was actually termed by one of Breuer's celebrated cases, Anna O, who used it to describe how she was freed from her neurotic symptoms.

Freud was a devotee of both Charcot and Breuer, and collaborated with both of them during his early career. Breuer and Freud called the hypnotic effect 'catharsis' (Greek for 'cleansing' or discharging).

Psychoanalysis

Psychoanalysis was Freud's development of the earlier work. He strove to understand the hidden world of the mind, the 'unconscious'. He formulated his theory that it was not the hypnotic state which was responsible for the cure of the patient, but the therapeutic relationship of the doctor and patient, working together. Thus, the patient was able to be 'cured' in the conscious state.

One of the methods he used to gain access to the unconscious mind was through dream interpretation. Freud called dreams 'the royal road to the unconscious'; that is, they are the most direct route for understanding what is happening inside the different levels of the unconscious mind.

Another method Freud used for reaching the unconscious was 'free association'. The patient was encouraged to say anything which came into their mind, which would trigger the hidden memories which were being repressed. Freud helped them interpret the results. Through insight (understanding) into their painful earlier experiences, Freud's patients were able to become psychologically healthier.

Many people discredit Freud's work because of one of his early theories; that a child has repressed sexual interest in its parents, and has to overcome this fantasy relationship before it can mature into adulthood. He genuinely believed that, when children reported they had been sexually abused by their parents, they were fantasising as a result of this repressed interest. Thus Freud was ultimately responsible for endless psychological damage not only to his own patients, but also to those of other exponents of his theory over the years. Freud later discarded this theory. One cannot discount the many other areas in which Freud threw light on the workings of the unconscious mind.

I have included some useful URLs of websites in chapter 11, which will give you far more detail about psychoanalysis.

Analytical Psychology

Jung was concerned about the ability of a person to become an individual, and to develop value and meaning in his life; he called this process 'individuation'. He theorised that an individual person consists of many different personalities, or 'archetypes'. By understanding these sub personalities, and integrating them, the personality would become balanced and psychologically whole.

Jung also developed the theory of the 'collective unconscious' which was the common human experiences of mankind throughout history, expressed by the many different cultural myths.

If you read mythology, you will notice, as Jung did, that many of the stories in different cultures are similar. For example, the Christian story of a man, born of a virgin, who was killed and then resurrected is a common 'hero' myth in many of the world mythologies. Myths are representations of common human experiences, such as the cycles of love and death.

Jung proposed the theory of different 'psychological types', notably 'introverts' (persons who are inward looking, reflective) and 'extroverts' (those who are more worldly, sociable), and the variations upon these. This was the beginning of 'psychology' as a science.

Jung was very interested in religion and philosophy, and studied these subjects deeply. He felt that it was essential for men to have a 'mythological' or 'spiritual' dimension to their life, in order to be fully human. For example, he noticed the serenity of the Pueblo Indians, who believed that by carrying out daily rites they could ensure that the sun would continue its passage across the sky. Believing they were a part of the cycle of existence gave them inner confidence and serenity.

Psychotherapy
All modern psychotherapies stem from the original teachings of Freud and Jung. It is impossible within one book to explain the workings of even a small part of these fascinating therapies, but they have some common areas.

The psychotherapies are all 'talking' cures, in that the patient/client (which ever term you prefer) speaks, writes, acts, or otherwise communicates his difficulties to the therapist verbally. Usually, the therapist will assist the patient to 'interpret' the problems, and come to an understanding as to why that problem occurred originally.

Psychology
Psychology is the study of human behaviour, and has its roots in Jung's work. Psychologists study human behaviour, and conduct extensive research to scientifically quantify the effectiveness of psychological therapy. It is probably easier to give a practical example of their work in practice. A person who is afraid of spiders (arachnophobia) for example, might be worked with on two levels. The Psychologist might help them to discover why they are fearful of this small creature; perhaps it represents something evil or perhaps spiders are linked with something bad in their earlier life.

On the second, and very practical level, the Psychologist might help the patient to draw up a plan to gradually desensitise their fear. The patient will be encouraged to look at drawings or photographs of real spiders, to touch the photograph, to look at a spider which has been confined in a glass, and as an ultimate test, to touch a spider. All of this process can take several weeks or months to achieve.

Counselling
Counselling is becoming a recognised profession, with better training and a wide range of people practising. Counsellors can be found in

many settings; Universities, Corporates, G.P. Surgeries, as well as in private practice.

The roots of counselling lie in the old village wise women and North American Indian 'pow-wow's, where the troubled person was allowed to talk about problems which had occurred within the Community. In the former case, the seeker talked with the wise woman on her own; in the latter, the whole community turned out to listen and offer advice (the forerunner of group therapy?). Counselling, like any of the psychotherapies, can take any of many forms, according to training and practice.

Summary of Chapter 5

Is a mental illness the result of brain chemistry imbalance
Electro Convulsive Therapy (ECT)
Drug Therapies
Designing and Marketing New Drugs
Categories of Drugs for Sale
Psychosurgery
Psychological/ Psychotherapy/ Counselling – the 'talking cures'

CHAPTER 6

The Medical Therapists

This Chapter includes:
What is a 'Therapist'?
How Does someone Choose A Therapist?
Do Therapists Have Problems?
Length of time training
Personal Experience – Vital for therapists?
Choosing a Therapist – 'Empathy'
Why Do Therapists Become Therapists?

The second part of this chapter contains:
an alphabetical listing of Therapists *
theory and methodology
a 'day in the life of' each Therapist

Counsellor	Psychiatrist
General Practitioner	Clinical Psychologist
Mental Nurse	Psychotherapist
Occupational Therapist	Rehabilitation Officer
Pharmacist	Social Worker
	Hypnotherapists & Hypno-Psychotherapists

What is a 'Therapist'?

A "therapy" according to my battered Oxford Illustrated Dictionary, is 'a curative medical treatment'. A 'Therapist' is therefore one who gives out such treatment. One could argue that it strictly applies only to medically trained personnel, but here I am using the term loosely to describe people who are paid professionally:

1.   to give curative treatment to patients with a mental illness;

or

2.   to assist their client's personal development

How Does someone Choose A Therapist?

If a patient is referred to a Community Mental Health Team, then this decision is made for them. The Team meets to discuss new referrals, and decides who might be suitable and has space on their 'case list' to take new patients. People who choose to go privately can choose their own therapist. The secret of success is to find someone you respect. The method the therapist uses is secondary to the fact that their therapy must work for you.

Do Therapists Have Problems?

Those who have learned to deal with their own life problems make the best Therapists. Therapists who have not dealt with their own problems can still be effective, as long as they are in current therapy themselves. Therapists who have problems and do not realize it are not really helping their clients.

Length of time training

This varies hugely, but remember when considering this:
- Therapists starting their career at an earlier age will have less 'life experience' and therefore will need extra training
- In general, longer term therapies are used to treat problems of long standing
- In general, shorter term therapies are used to treat problems of shorter duration
- the relationship developed between client (patient) and therapist is as important as the training, perhaps more so.

Personal Experience – Vital for therapists?

Imagine taking your Ford car to a mechanic. His theoretical training has been excellent; he has repaired cars during his training. He will repair it adequately no doubt. Imagine, your car is a Porsche, and your mechanic races these cars, has re-built his own, including the engine – in other words, he is a Specialist with personal experience.

Considering the value of your car, to whom would you entrust the repairs?

Choosing a Therapist – 'Empathy'

As well as considering which specialist will best be capable of dealing with your particular need, you need to consider, does the Therapist appear to have a deep understanding of your problem. How will you know this? They may or may not be willing to share their own experiences, but you can test the degree of their 'empathy' by asking yourself:

- How do I feel towards them –
  e.g. do I feel warmth and is it reciprocated
- When I give them examples do they seem to understand?

Why Do Therapists Become Therapists?

Why would someone choose to work in this profession? It is often not well paid, the hours are erratic, and the work is often distressing. Patients leave therapy and are never seen again and may be only silently grateful; patients who complain are vociferous.

Someone who has that not easily defined quality we call 'empathy', or ability to understand someone else' suffering, will make a good Therapist and enjoy their work.

Our Therapists

Let's make this a bit more real by giving our Therapists a name. The Therapists marked 👪 work in a Mental Health or Primary Care Team; the Therapists marked 👤 work generally in private practice. The Therapists additionally marked 👤 are medically or scientifically trained i.e. they either prescribe, dispense, or administer drugs.

Team staff sometimes choose to work privately as well. Let's give them some names (the syringe symbol denotes a medical training);

♀	Counsellor	Vera	
♀♀♀	General Practitioner	Dr. Mason	ⷮ
♀♀♀	Mental Nurse	Adrian	ⷮ
♀♀♀	Occupational Therapist	Petra	
♀	Pharmacist	John Jethro	ⷮ
♀♀♀	Psychiatrist	Paul Lacey	
♀	Psycho Analyst	Peter	
♀♀♀	Psychotherapist	Alison	
♀♀♀	Psychologist	Anna	
♀♀♀	Rehabilitation Worker	Marlene	
♀♀♀	Social Worker	Eric	

For some reason, although most people are on first name terms, Doctors were generally referred to by their title and surname. "Mr" is a title which Surgeons and other Consultants generally use.

Counsellors

Theory Training & Methodology
There are many different types of counselling, each with their own pet theory which attempts to explain how problems can be resolved. Each "School" will have specific training, which may take between one and four years.

Some schools favour individual counselling, others therapy within groups; some believe the dynamics of the relationship between

71

individuals is paramount, whilst other feel that social interaction that is at the core of 'cure'. Some schools tackle problems head on, using behavioural methods, whilst others feel that insight is the key to change.

Trainees must not have too many pre-conceptions about particular beliefs, as they to be able to accept whatever is presented by their clients – dogmatists do not make good Counsellors. They must also have a very strong ethical system to which they adhere.

A budding Counsellor will have to prove that he/she has the necessary characteristics to deal with distressed people, without becoming distressed. They must be creative in their approach, and ready to accept whatever their clients bring with compassion and understanding. All good Counsellors have supervision from other professionals and also receive therapy themselves on a regular basis.

Type of Client
The type of problem referred to a Counsellor varies a great deal – bereavement, depressive illness, or someone who has a specific, time limited life problem they need to resolve, all respond well to this therapy.

Supportive counselling may be offered to clients with major mental illness, and to their carers; that is, counselling which does not attempt to extract the root of the problem, but seeks to offer emotional and practical support. Counsellors explain to their clients that therapy can often be as painful as it is revealing, and that they have to be prepared to make changes in their life, if they want to learn from their therapeutic experiences.

A Day in the Life of Vera, a Counsellor
Vera is a Counsellor in Brief Therapy. She works in private practice, and additionally for a group of General Practitioners.

In private practice, Vera has to spend a good deal of time advertising her services to find clients, and visiting potential suppliers of clients. She obtains private referrals from GP's as well as seeing their patients on a contractual basis.

Vera produces monthly accounts, sends out invoices, and writes her own brochures and sales literature. All of these administrative tasks, coupled with her own supervision and further professional training will mean working far more than a standard 37 hour week.

Vera arrives at her rooms in the surgery for the first session of the day. Her client Tom does not arrive on time, but Vera has to wait in case he is late. Almost 30 minutes later, he arrives apologetically; he had forgotten about the appointment. Vera has to be firm about not letting him take more than his allotted time, or she will be late for her next patient.

Tom wants to talk about the possibility of a separation from his wife. They are no longer in love. Tom has a daughter of 9 years, and he is anxious about the effect the planned separation will have on her.

Tom talks to Vera, and she listens – sometimes making a comment if she feels he needs to clarify a point. The purpose of the session is not for Vera to give advice, but to help Tom clarify his thoughts, gain insights and to make his own decisions.

At the end of the Session, Tom is quite clear that he should separate, but needs to think about how best to provide for his family and himself during what will be a difficult time. Vera might see Tom for up to 6 'sessions', each of these lasting about one hour, during which they have agreed to 'work' on his feelings about the ending of his marriage.

Vera's second client, Jean, is anxious about the disappearance of her daughter. In this session, Vera does not interrupt her non-stop stream of words. Jean is less anxious when she leaves, as she has had the opportunity of airing her feelings. Sometimes it works like this, sometimes Counselling is a much more two way communication.

Her third client is undergoing a mid life crisis; Maggie is seeking a new career, but has a range of problems with her teenage children, which are taking up a great deal of her time. Maggie is not distressed, but needs guidance. Vera teaches this client how to resolve problems using a 6-step approach.

After a brief break, during which she has to see a hostile Practice Manager about problems with noise outside the room, Vera goes back to her home/office to see two private clients before setting down to the outstanding administrative work. Time for a coffee and to read the paper first.

She sighs as she sees the accounts and a pile of Case Notes which need completion. She has to keep case notes about each client, which contain information about the client's problems, the family background, and the proposed treatment. The case notes are discussed with the supervisor in general terms, but are highly confidential and not seen by anyone else.

She is about to make the coffee when the phone rings – it is one of the General Practitioners from the Surgery. He is worried about one of his patients, and wants Vera to see the gentleman quickly. Vera manages to find a free spot in her diary for the next day; she usually keeps a free appointment for such emergencies.

Vera's final appointment of the day is to visit her Supervisor, whom she sees twice a week. During these sessions, she receives important feedback about the quality of her work. The Supervisor is also able to judge whether or not Vera is 'mentally' fit herself. Vera has to pay for the Supervision out of her client fees; she also pays for private

Counselling sessions for herself, and is looking forward to Wednesday when her own appointment is due.

Relaxation is important for all Therapists. Vera likes to relax by watching old movies. She likes the old Hammer horror films, and anything science fiction. Vera will probably not spend all of her career counselling, as private practice can be quite stressful; she is thinking about using her knowledge to write some Therapeutic books, and perhaps doing some teaching.

General Practitioners

Theory Training & Methodology

"General Practitioners", as they are professionally known, are just as their official title describes. They are people who have taken a lengthy course (about 7 years in total, consisting both of examinations and practical 'on-the-job' training in hospitals), and practice 'general medicine'.

General Practitioners are taught the "medical model" of seeing patients problems, that is, they are taught how to use medicines (therapeutic drugs) to cure their patients illnesses. Some of them take additional training in psychiatric medicine, which teaches them about the therapeutic use of drugs in psychiatric medicine. Others may additionally train in counselling or psychotherapy, but this is less common. Others may take additional training and become Surgeons.

Competition for Medical School is high, and they have to achieve good science grades if they want to be accepted for training as Medical Doctors (an "MBBS" degree). General Practitioners are trained in the sciences; they all study anatomy, physiology and biology, as well as specialising later on in their own areas of interest if they so wish.

The term "Doctor" actually refers to a Degree, or Doctorate, which has been conferred as a result of successfully passing an examination; in this case, Doctor of Medicine ("MD"). The term 'Doctor' is used colloquially– e.g. "I went to my Doctor the other day" (as opposed to "I went to my Mechanic the other day....); but strictly speaking this is an incorrect use of the term.

Type of Client
GPs deal in general medicine, and see patients with a very broad range of complaints. Patients refer themselves to their practitioners for all sorts of things, including both physical and mental illnesses, and physical problems.

If a GP feels that he needs further advice for a particular patient, then he might refer them on to a specialist. Specialists do not generally see patients unless a GP has made a specific referral. There are specialists who deal with most of the parts of the body, for example cardiac, ear nose and throat, gynaecologists, orthodontists. A GP retains clinical responsibility for his patient, even if that person is referred on to a specialist, which means that in law he is responsible for the physical well-being of his patient. You might consider the awesome responsibility of this task, particularly in the case of the potentially suicidal patient.

You may notice that Counsellors often refer to 'clients', whereas a Doctor will use the term 'patient'. This is just a protocol, in the same way that surgeons take the honorary title of 'Mr' rather than 'Dr'.

A Day in the Life of Dr Mason, a General Practitioner
Dr. Mason is a General Practitioners in his late 40's. He is the most senior G.P. at his surgery. He is qualified to prescribe drugs, and to treat wounds and illnesses. He does not perform surgical operations, nor does he practice Psychiatry.

Dr Mason usually has a morning Surgery, for which his patients will make specific appointments. Surgery starts at 8.30 am, but Dr Mason often arrives before that to clear some of his administrative work. Many NHS forms are required for each patient he sees.

As each patient arrives for their appointment, the Receptionist finds their notes, and hand them to Dr Mason. The case notes act as a clinical record and memory aid; a GP will not remember all the details about a patient and their medications. Some GPs use a computer to record their clinical records. All visits, medications, and other information about the patient have to be recorded by law. Dr Mason is aware that his patients have the right to see their notes, so he is careful not to write anything which could be misinterpreted.

The Surgery is so busy that Dr Mason has to limit each patient to 10 minutes, during which has to find out what the patient wants by conducting an interview. He will diagnose and then prescribe suitable medications or perhaps suggest psychological treatment.

He usually completes his notes before he sees the next patient. He leaves 2 appointments at the end of his Surgery clear, in case a patient rings and needs an urgent appointment.

When his final patient of morning Surgery leaves (about 11.30am), Dr Mason completes further paperwork, prints out repeat prescriptions, signs forms, and answers any questions from his colleagues about other patients. He generally sees representatives from Drug companies after morning surgery. They advise him of any new drugs which have completed clinical trials and are available for sale.

Dr Mason is involved in Clinical Trials for two new drugs, and has to complete forms for each patient on his list who is a part of the trial. (see diagrams 4a 4b 4c in Chapter 5).

Dr. Mason spends the rest of his time before lunch overseeing training for Junior Doctors, who will work at the Surgery as part of their training. He will generally employ a Practice Manager to look after the bulk of the general administration for the Surgery.

In the afternoon he sits in on a practice meeting with his colleagues, where they discuss their patients and any matters relating to the surgery.

During evening surgery, which runs from about 6.00pm, Dr Mason sees another eleven patients, before going home to his family. Tonight, he is on emergency callout, which means he has to be available if one of his patients calls during the night. He covers emergency callout about twice a month, and additionally has to work late when one of his colleagues is off sick, and he cannot find a replacement locum.

He finds it difficult to unwind after a busy day, but enjoys Classical music concerts and the odd game of golf. Many GPs divorce under the strain of the long and often unsociable hours and Dr Mason wants to take steps to make sure that does not happen to him, so he tries whenever possible to call in extra help rather than taking on all the extra hours himself.

Mental Nurses

Theory Training & Methodology
Registered Mental Nurses take a 3 year training course, some of this in the classroom, and some on-the-job. They are taught how to recognise the symptoms of major mental illnesses, and various forms of therapy, possibly behavioural therapies. They are taught the various theories for the causes of mental illness, generally the 'medical model' which teaches drug therapy. Nurses generally accept that mental illnesses

depression, mania and bi polar illness are caused by an imbalance in the brain chemistry.

At the end of their training, they are qualified to administer drugs by mouth and injection, although only a GP or Psychiatrist can prescribe the drugs. They also are able to diagnose mental illness, under the Supervision of a Consultant Psychiatrist.

Mental Nurses work in a community mental health team, usually attached to a local Psychiatric Hospital, sometimes visiting patients in their homes, sometimes receiving them at the clinic. They keep clinical records, in the same way as other therapists, and attend meetings of the community mental health team, where they discuss patients with other team members.

Type of Client

Mental Nurses have a caseload consisting of patients with long-term mental illness, who need regular medication and psychological support. Additionally, they are referred patients who are suffering short term problems and anxieties, similar to the patients referred to Counsellors, though this is less their speciality.

They administer 'depot' injections to patients who require long-term medication; these are injections into the buttocks or back of the hand, which are given about monthly, and alleviate the needle pain a patient might experience with daily injections.

A Day in the Life of Adrian, a Mental Nurse

Adrian sees patients in the Community, and diagnoses mental illness, though he is responsible clinically to both a Senior Nurse and a Consultant. He is trained in all aspects of mental illness, and carries out therapeutic work both inside and outside the Hospital.

As a Nurse, Adrian is responsible for helping to train junior Nurses, a part of his work he enjoys. He is currently studying for a Degree in Nursing, and takes some time out during the day to write his essays.

Adrian's first patient is Stan, who has a long-term mental illness, and needs a regular depot injection. Stan was diagnosed with schizophrenia about 10 years ago. Stan's medication enables him to live a fairly normal life, and he goes out to work every day.

Adrian likes to see Stan once a fortnight to support him socially, as Stan lives on his own. Some patients see either Social Workers, Occupational Therapists, or Rehabilitation Officer instead, but as Adrian already sees Stan regularly for depots, he feels that it is better to give Stan the reassurance of being visited by the same person.

As it is a Wednesday, Adrian has to attend the weekly Team meeting. He has prepared short reports on all of his clients. Adrian asks for advice on two particular cases, and asks the Social Worker to visit Stan to help him complete some tax forms.

Adrian takes on two new clients referred by the Primary Health Care Team. He asks Marlene the Rehabilitation Officer to see the second client with him. 'Cross disciplinary work', in which more than one Team member sees a particular patient, is quite common.

After the meeting, Adrian has coffee with his colleagues in the Team. He is attending his weekly session with his Supervisor, a Senior Mental Nurse, after this.

During this Session, his Senior Nurse notices that Adrian is looking stressed, and comments on it. He asks Adrian if he is sure he can cope with the extra two people on his list. Adrian is relieved, and agrees that perhaps he is taking on too much. The senior works with Adrian to rearrange his diary, spacing some of the appointments further apart, and leaving some room for emergency 'Sections'. His senior also suggests that Adrian books some of his holidays.

After lunch, Adrian calls to Mrs Abrahams, who is suffering panic attacks. She has recently been bereaved of her teenage daughter, and she and her husband are finding it hard to come to terms with the loss. Adrian feels that bereavement Counselling will be beneficial to both of them, and arranges an appointment with CRUSE on their behalf.

Adrian does not feel too good himself, and decides to take the advice of his senior, cancels the two remaining appointments of the afternoon, and goes home early. If he is not feeling well himself, then he will not be of much use to his clients. Perhaps that holiday might be a good idea.

Occupational Therapists

Theory Training & Methodology
The title for this role in the Team is a little misleading; their role in mental health may include far more than just a patient's occupation. They also assess patients who have physical or mental disabilities, in order to provide practical aids which will enable them to live independent lives within the community. They become involved with:
- assessing the physical disabilities of their patient
- prescribing practical aids e.g. bathing aids, chair hoists
- assisting their patients to find suitable "occupation" (employment or leisure time)
- assessing conditions for welfare benefit application purposes (a role they share with the Social Workers and Rehabilitation Workers)

Trained for 3 years, they also learn about the various aspects of mental health, although they are not medically trained nor do they prescribe medications.

Type of Client

As we are dealing with mental health, our particular therapist is a specialist in people who have both mental and physical disability, although many Occupational Therapists will deal specifically with the latter.

Depending on the number and type of therapists in her team, she may also be called upon to look after clients who do not have a specific disability, but who might benefit from practical guidance and support, such as someone living alone who has a long-term depressive illness and needs social support. The roles therefore cross the boundaries between a Social Worker and a Rehabilitation Therapist, although this is not the main aim of the training.

A Day in the Life of Petra, an Occupational Therapist

Petra spends much of her time in patient's homes. On today's first visit, she is helping her client Gina to overcome agoraphobia. Petra has been working on a programme which will enable Gina to gradually, over a period of a few months, to walk from her house and visit her sister, who lives about a mile away. Petra is being supervised by the Clinical Psychologist in the team, who specialises in such 'behavioural therapy'.

On each visit, Petra and Gina will walk further from Gina's house, until she is able to walk alone to her sister's house, where Petra will meet her. Today, they have managed to get Gina 100 yards from her front door; this may not seem a large achievement, but it has taken Gina 10 years to get this far. It is not easy. Some people with agoraphobia remain indoors for large portions of their life.

After leaving Gina, Petra drives back to her Team room, to complete some Case Notes and call the Social Security Office regarding an application for disability benefit. She talks to some colleagues over lunch, and then finishes off her notes, before driving to her next appointment, with Vanya.

Vanya was crippled in a car crash two years ago. Vanya is still trying to come to terms with the emotional and physical realities of life in a wheel chair. She is on the case list of the Mental Health Team, as the stress of the crash triggered a bout of depressive illness.

Vanya has asked Petra to look at the equipment in her kitchen and living room. She is finding it difficult to manoeuvre her wheelchair into the kitchen, and whilst there, finds it hard to grasp items of food she is preparing. Petra knows the various aids which are on the market, and when she has finished her assessment, she can talk to Vanya about what is available.

Petra is beginning to feel tired; she has to collect her son from Nursery School in an hour, and still has another call to make, to see Arthur. She decides to shorten the next visit, and makes some space in her diary to see Arthur the following week.

Petra is due to run a class tomorrow for long term mentally ill patients who want to learn to basic cooking and home making skills. For some patients, their illness makes concentration and remembering difficult; mental suffering uses a great deal of available mental and intellectual energy. Petra has to take this into account when running these courses for example she may teach her class how to prepare a meal from ready prepared ingredients rather than from scratch.

She collects her son, then goes home to prepare their tea, her notes for the course, and to write up her case notes for the day. She is a divorcee and has to be well organized to fit in her work with her life as a mother; but at least she understands some of the frustrations and difficulties of those of her clients who are single mothers.

Pharmacists

Theory Training & Methodology

Pharmacists are highly qualified scientists, who specialise in the preparation and dispensing of medicines (drugs). Their profession dates back to the early Nineteenth Century, when practitioners were variously known by the quaint sounding names of 'Apothecaries', or 'Druggists'; or perhaps 'Chemists'. They work in Research Laboratories, Hospitals, or Community Pharmacies.

Students with excellent passes in science subjects such as chemistry and physics take a four-year Master of Pharmacy honours degree course (plus one year post degree training). Among the subjects they study are:

- the physical properties of chemicals
- chemistry as applied to pharmaceuticals (drugs used as medicines)
- the reaction of these chemicals in the human body
- how to measure the correct dose of each drug
- advising on the treatment of minor ailments

Pharmacists are currently not allowed by law to prescribe drugs and medication, which is the province of the G.P. They can override a GP's prescription for drugs, where the Pharmacist has reason to believe that the GP has prescribed wrongly, or has proposed a drug which is incompatible with other medication the patient might be taking. Scientifically, Pharmacists are more qualified in the chemical side of drugs than G.Ps.

Type of Client

Pharmacists' customers can be from all walks of life, and suffering either physical or mental disorders. Customers can obtain their medications from either a 'Chemist's Shop', or maybe a pharmacy within a supermarket store. Although Pharmacists cannot prescribe drugs, they can advise their customers on what they consider is the correct drug for their complaint and indeed many of them enjoy this community aspect of their work.

A customer might ask a Pharmacist to recommend the most suitable drug or proprietary medicine from the huge array which can be sold 'over the counter'.

A Day in the Life of John Jethro, Community based Pharmacist

John's Pharmacy is in a 'Chemist's Shop', where he also sells medicines off-the-counter. In the shop, he has several assistants, who run the shop and till. By law, he has to be in the shop when medicines are dispensed, in case his customers need to ask questions about how the medication has to be taken:

- with or without food
- number of times a day
- if any foodstuffs are specifically 'contra-indicate' with the medicines;
  i.e.
  - some foods react with the medicines and make it ineffective
  - some foods are dangerous when taken with certain medicines

It is 9.00am Friday, and the Chemists' Shop is about to open. John Jethro has not yet arrived. Sally, one of the assistants, serves a customer with toiletries, but the lady then asks for a specific cold sore preparation. Sally knows that she is not legally allowed to sell this medicine unless the Pharmacist is on the premises. Her customer is annoyed, but Sally is firm. Luckily, John arrives, and he is able to dispense the required medicine.

The shop is already becoming busy, and John retires into the Pharmacy to mix up some tablets for one of his regular customers. Most of the pills he dispenses are made commercially, but occasionally one of the local G.P.'s prescribes a medication which is not available in the required strength, and has to be made up especially. He loves this part of his work; it reminds him of his days in the chemistry labs at college.

Two more Assistants have arrived, leaving Sally free at the Counter. Fridays are good days for stock taking, and John finishes the prescription of pills, and runs through the Sally's stock list for the following week. As it is autumn, he decides to have more stocks of the influenza and cold medicines; he knows through experience which are more popular and therefore more likely to sell. John has to be a businessman too.

John has given Sally the job of checking the dates on all the products on the shelves; the out of date ones have to be destroyed. They make up an order to each of the large suppliers, which Sally sends through by fax or telephone each week.

After lunch, Bill (a representative from one of the Pharmaceutical firms) arrives with some new samples of headache and asthma cures, and John goes into the back office with him to talk about some of the products for sale. John decides to purchase a small stock of a new drug which he believes will sell well.

Just as the Representative is leaving, the telephone rings. The local Hospital have a cancer patient who needs a certain drug, and their supplies are exhausted. The Pharmacist they usually contact has been called away on an emergency. John dispenses the necessary supplies, and hands it to the motorcycle courier, who has been commissioned to transport the drugs back to the Hospital.

All drugs of this nature have to be carefully accounted for with accurate paper records of the dispensing. This prevents them getting into the wrong hands. John adds a supply of the drug to the replenishment order which his Assistant is about to place.

John spends the rest of the afternoon making up prescriptions for callers to the shop, then visits Dr Mason with some drug orders, and stays for a few minutes while they enjoy a brief chat about the local football team.

6.00 pm, and the shop is officially closed, but John and Sally are still busy. John has to complete his paperwork on the drugs dispensed during the day. He also generally uses this time to attend to the 'scripts' (prescription drugs) of the local drug addicts. These are the addicts who are trying to wean themselves off hard drugs like heroin or cocaine, with the help of their G.P. or someone from the Psychiatric Hospital.

The addicts are prescribed legal chemical substitutes (such as methadone) which will lessen some of the worse effects (e.g. cramps, hallucinations) of coming off hard drugs. Some of the addicts are so desperate for their 'scripts' that they need to be allowed in the shop outside normal trading hours. John realizes that the addicts behaviour or appearance can upset his day-to-day customers, and protects his continued business by dispensing at special times.

It is 6.45pm, and at last he puts on the alarms (dangerous drugs are kept on the premises) and locks up. John is looking forward to a half-day's lecture he is giving over the weekend, to trainee Pharmacists at the local University. He is looking forward to the day when Pharmacists can prescribe drugs, and he can gain proper public recognition for his pharmaceutical training.

Psychiatrists

Theory Training & Methodology
A Psychiatrist is a specialist in mental health and psychiatric drugs. They train in General Medicine, and have obtained a Doctorate. After qualifying, they usually spend a year in General Practice, before taking

an extra 6 months training to enable them to become Junior Psychiatrists. It will then take up to 5 years to become a Consultant Psychiatrist.

Psychiatrists are taught that mental illnesses are caused by 'chemical disturbances' in the brain and therefore use drugs to treat mental illness in a chemical way. Serious illnesses such as chronic clinical depressive illness, mania, and schizophrenia will be treated in this manner. Some Psychiatrists have additional training in Psychological or Psychotherapeutic treatments, and practicing both methods.

Type of Client
A Psychiatrist sees a wide range of patients with mental health problems. They also treat organic (physical) brain disorders such as mental handicap and Alzheimer's disease, as well as patients who have sustained brain injuries. Many of these patients receive specific psychiatric drugs. Patients who refer with milder depressive illnesses, personality disorders, phobias, or social problems are likely be treated with psychological therapies in addition to medications. Patients with severe depressive illness will sometimes be treated by a course of ECT (electro convulsive therapy).

A Day in the Life of Dr Paul Lacey, a Consultant Psychiatrist
Dr Lacey's patients have appointments ranging from ½ hour to one hour, which is considerably longer than the 10 minutes allotted to a General Practitioner's patients. Psychiatrists not only assess patients for mental health; they will also carry out the therapeutic work.

Paul Lacey also deals with what are called 'forensic' cases, that is, people who are classed as criminals, and also have a mental illness. He might have to deal with paedophilia as well as psychopathic illness. Paul views them as people who are severely ill.

8.30 am, and he is already looking at the list of patients who have appointments. His list is full, and consists not only of appointments in the Psychiatric Hospital, but also community visits, and visits to the local prison.

First visit of the day is to Gannoway Prison, where he is to see Mac. Mac is an habitual alcoholic in his 60's, who is not expected to live for long. Mac suffers from schizophrenia. He stabbed and severely wounded his brother, under the delusion that his brother was an alien who was going to kill him.

Mac is in prison because there is nowhere else suitable for him to go. The secure hospital 20 miles away has no beds, and there are none either at the smaller unit in the local Psychiatric Hospital. The large Asylum closed under the Care in the Community Act, leaving very few resources available for people like Mac, who forgets to take his medication unless closely supervised.

Paul has a soft spot for Mac, who is quite a likeable character when 'normal'. Mac is a good cartoonist, and is drawing when Paul enters his cell – a portrait of a devil and an angel, in grey and blue chalks. Paul tries to persuade Mac to take a depot injection, and eventually Mac agrees.

Mac likes being in prison, because he feels secure there. He has no home of his own, and he knows the 'screws' (Prison Officers) well and regards them as his family. Mac feels quite lonely, as his family have refused to visit him, and hopes that at his next prison review he will not be given parole. He is likely to commit another offence if released, so that he can stay in the security of the prison.

Next call is back at the Hospital, where Dr Lacey is running a Seminar for some of the Junior Doctors. He enjoys training. There are some good new ideas from the trainees, as well as some amusing incidents.

One of the Trainees is convinced that a new 'therapy' has cured a long term patient. Paul knows the patient in question has been experiencing 'cures' for 20 years; but he does not like to dampen the obvious enthusiasm of the trainee. He suggests his student 'observes' the patient longer, before making conclusions. Training concludes 1½ hours later, and Paul goes back to his office to sign letters and see if his Secretary has had any calls.

An anxious Mental Nurse hurries toward him in the corridor, and asks him to see her patient, who is in the next room. The person in question is suffering a bout of severe depression, and is not responding to questions. Paul makes an unscheduled visit.

The lady, Pamela, is sitting on the floor, her head in her hands. She is distraught. By gentle questioning, Paul ascertains that her partner has left her, and she is unable to cope. She now has financial and housing worries on top of her original problems, and it is overwhelming her. Paul offers reassurance, and arranges for a Social Worker to call to her home.

Paul is now late for his next appointment, with a lady who is suffering mania. This is a very distressing illness, not only for the patient, but also her family. This lady, Marcia, is accompanied by her daughter, Ann.

Ann is very distressed. Her mother, during the height of her mania, has taken £8,000 out of her bank account, and given it to a very dubious charity. Marcia is extolling the virtues of the charity, while her daughter is crying. Ann tells Paul that her mother is behind with her mortgage payments, and is likely to lose the family home.

Paul is unable to stop Marcia talking, and sees she is getting deeper into her manic episode. He cannot section her under the Mental Health Act, as her current actions cannot be considered a 'danger to her life', despite very ruinous financial implications. In this respect, the Act has severe limitations. However, he does persuade Marcia to have an immediate injection of Haloperidol, which will reduce her manic levels.

After helping Ann get Marcia safely to bed, and talking to Ann for a while about some social support from Adrian (the Social Worker), Paul leaves.

Late afternoon, and he is in his office writing case notes, and also lecture notes for the student doctors. Each week he likes to attend the Journal Club, which gives advanced training to Junior Doctors, and is one of the few occasions where they can meet up with their peers during the working day.

Paul sometimes works very late, but this evening he has promised to attend a family event, and has made sure his diary is free. On his days off, Paul likes to swim and play golf. He finds it hard to fit in the work he loves, within the confines of having a large family (4 children, all under 9 years). He has to be careful that his marriage does not suffer under the strain of the long working hours which are unfortunately a normal part of his routine.

Psycho Analysts

Theory Training & Methodology
Psycho Analysts (followers of Sigmund Freud) are a very rare breed and therefore generally have long waiting lists. Their training is long and expensive, and each Analyst has to undergo a training analysis. To train a good Analyst is reckoned to take about 10 years.

Psycho = of the mind; analysis = investigation. An analyst will investigate the sick (neurotic) mind by analysing what has gone wrong with the mental processes (thinking). Analysts believe that when their patient become aware of their unconscious mental processes, they are then in a position to understand and deal with their life difficulties.

As the mental processes cannot be 'seen', this type of Therapist will have to get information from the patient:

- Expressed emotions - the kind of emotions expressed when talking about specific subjects e.g. are they angry or happy when talking about parents or brothers
- Thoughts - patients are allowed to 'free associate' (talk freely without interruption) and thus will often inadvertently reveal vital facts of which they might be consciously unaware
- Fantasies and dreams – Freudians belief that dreams are the mind's way of revealing otherwise unacceptable facts or situations

Trainee Psycho-Analysts have to spend some years being psycho-analysed themselves, before they are allowed their own patients. If you consider the complexity of human thinking and behaviour, and how difficult it is to look at oneself from a distant perspective, then you might begin to understand why this treatment type of treatment takes so long.

Patients will be expected to attend from 2 to 4 sessions a week, each session lasting about 45 minutes (a 'therapeutic hour'). The last 15 minutes of the time is used by the Analyst to complete his case notes.

Type of Client

An analyst will see a variety of patients, generally people who are intelligent and wish to learn more about themselves and how to conduct their lives more productively. It is a therapy which teaches people to understand themselves and gain insights.

Analysis can be very expensive, so a patient has to have sufficient private income to sustain the large number of sessions required. It is generally not available on the NHS because of the costs and time involved.

A Day in the Life of Peter, a Psycho Analyst

Peter takes his dog for a walk first thing each morning – to clear and refresh his mind before starting work.

Peter is due to see his first patient, Stella, at 9.30am. She sees him twice a week, for about 45 minutes. Stella has been his patient for 3 years now, and is about to conclude her therapy. She referred herself to Peter originally after a very unhappy childhood, followed by an unhappy marriage. During the marriage, Stella had lost all confidence in herself, and wanted to work with Peter to try to discover her hidden capabilities. She also wanted to find out why the marriage had not worked, so that if she married again, things might be different.

Stella has experienced many dreams during her analysis, which she has described to Peter. Through these dreams, which were sometimes quite violent, they have uncovered Stella's anger towards her father (now deceased), which she had been unconsciously (unaware) directing towards her husband. Stella was now realising that she had married a weak man, whom she could 'bully' in the way she was bullied by her father. Both Stella and Peter are hopeful that her next relationship will be built on a more equal footing.

Peter takes 15 minutes after Stella leaves to write up her notes. Some Analysts do not make notes during their time with their patient, relying on their memory. They feel that taking notes is intrusive, and they might also miss vital information.

His next patient is called Jester, a name which does not reflect his true feelings, as he is in reality a sad man, gradually recovering from a schizophrenic illness. Not many Medics feel that this illness can be treated with analysis, but Peter seems to be having remarkable success with Jester, an intelligent man who has been in analysis now for 5 years.

Peter and Jester have been analysing the latter's delusions, which centre around a bizarre circus and its performers. As a result, Jester's delusions are almost under control, and he is beginning to deal with the difficulties and emotions in real life.

As Jester leaves, Peter sees his third client of the day driving up the lane to his house. This is a new patient, Marilyn. She is early for her appointment. Peter signals out of the window that he has seen her and for her to wait in the lane. He does not like his incoming and outgoing patients to see each other, as that would breach his strict ethics on confidentiality.

Marilyn is cross at being kept waiting, and expresses this Peter by deliberately knocking one of his plants off the stand as she enters the room, then watches for his reaction. He smiles inwardly – is this how she expresses her anger in her every day life? The process of analysis begins.

Peter loves classical music, and lovingly draws his violin from its case. A little Mozart today, perhaps. He lives a very full life; he has learned from his patient's experiences how important that is for mental well being.

PRIMARY CARE & THE C.M.H.T. (Community Mental Health Team)

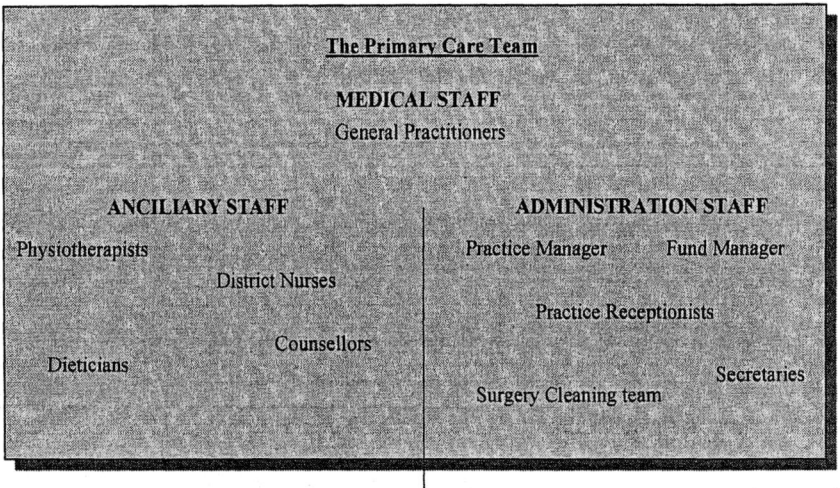

<u>The Primary Care Team</u>

MEDICAL STAFF
General Practitioners

ANCILIARY STAFF

Physiotherapists

District Nurses

Counsellors

Dieticians

ADMINISTRATION STAFF

Practice Manager   Fund Manager

Practice Receptionists

Surgery Cleaning team

Secretaries

PATIENT REFERRALS SENT TO TEAM, VIA TEAM LEADER

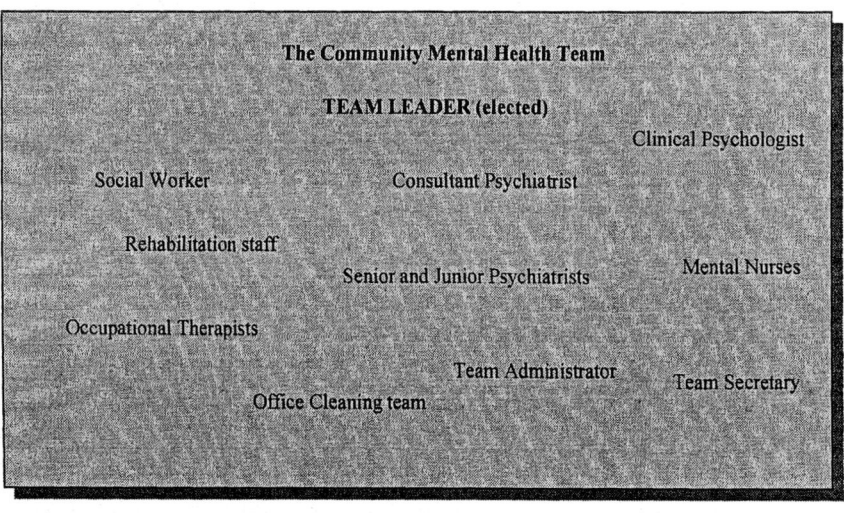

The Community Mental Health Team

TEAM LEADER (elected)

Clinical Psychologist

Social Worker   Consultant Psychiatrist

Rehabilitation staff

Senior and Junior Psychiatrists   Mental Nurses

Occupational Therapists

Team Administrator   Team Secretary

Office Cleaning team

Clinical Psychologists

Theory Training & Methodology

Psychology is the study of human behaviour; thinking 'patterns'. Psychologists are scientific in their methodology and carry out rigorous research into their work, using statistical analysis to determine how beneficial certain of their therapies are in practice. They publish professional papers about various aspects of their work, and carry out research on mental health issues. They also conduct research in the community, for example upon the social effects of mental illness in the families of patients.

Psychologists examine the facts relating to the patient's home and family life, and a whole host of life circumstances which might affect their patient's well-being (see Chapter 5 on Treatments). Psychology is designed to help patients understand themselves better, and change negative behaviours which are causing problems in their lives.

Psychologists often work together with Psychiatrists, and generally accept the medical model of 'chemical imbalance' in the brain. They will treat the patient psychologically, and might additionally work with Psychiatrists, who will prescribe medications to their patients.

Clinical Psychologists work in Hospitals. They have a long training, starting with 3 to 4 years to complete an Honours Degree in Psychology, then a further 3 years specialist training to become a Registered 'Clinical Psychologist'.

Type of Client

Clients with both severe mental illness and long standing life/relationship problems respond well to psychological methods, as do those with illnesses such as phobias, anxiety, and eating disorders.

Psychologists see their patients regularly over several months or years. People who have a degree of insight already, and work hard to understand and practice new behaviours, have very successful results with Psychologists.

A Day in the Life of Anna, a Clinical Psychologist

Anna, like many other trainees, had been very interested in human psychology from an early age; she had a difficult childhood, and an innate curiosity about why people behaved the way they did.

Jenny is the first patient of the day. Jenny has experienced great cruelty by her father in childhood, and now becomes very frightened at work when her male bosses criticize her, often bursting into tears, then becoming embarrassed at her own behaviour. She keeps making mistakes at work, and is beginning to lose her confidence. She is also becoming depressed.

Jenny is probably not aware that her childhood experience has a bearing on her current fear of men. Anna would term Jenny's behaviour towards men as being a 'negative behaviour pattern'.

Anna's job is to treat Jenny with 'behavioural psychology', assisting her to become aware of how her childhood patterns of behaviour (i.e. her fear of men) are being repeated in her adult situation at work. By bringing this 'repeated behaviour' (or 'behaviour pattern') to her patient's awareness, Jenny will be able to work towards different and more productive behaviour towards men in the future.

After Jenny, Anna goes onto the ward to see her long-term patients, most of whom are suffering from schizophrenia. Anna sees her role as trying to improve the daily life of these patients, by bringing order into their otherwise chaotic world. She devises programmes of social rehabilitation, which are carried out by an Occupational Therapist or Rehabilitation Worker. A structured programme is very beneficial socially and also comforting to a patient who has to cope with frightening delusions and hallucinations.

It is nearly lunch-time, and Anna goes to the staff canteen, where she meets up with some of her colleagues. It is very difficult for them to take a break, and not talk 'shop'. Anna devises a game, and looks in the car park to see how many cars of each colour are there today; she is keeping a log for amusement.

In the afternoon, Anna is on community visit to a patient with a severe depressive illness. The lady (Sandie) should be in hospital, but her husband is adamant that he wants to keep her at home at all costs, where he can keep an eye on her.

Anna spends time listening and sitting with Sandie, who is quiet and subdued. Sandie's husband Jack is worried. Anna feels it is important for him to be present although, like many men in this situation, he finds it very hard to cope with his wife's deep and lasting sad mood. Anna has explained to them why depressive illnesses are believed to occur, and how they are treated.

If Anna feels that her patient's life is in danger, then she will ask her to become an in-patient, either voluntarily as a preference, or else under a Section of The Mental Health Act. There are not many occasions on which she has had to invoke the latter, as she can be very persuasive!

After 1½ hours, which is a fairly long time in therapeutic terms, Anna finally leaves the house, and drives to her next appointment. She meets up with Eric (the Social Worker). They are visiting a man who is strongly suspected of the sexual abuse of his two grandchildren. This will be a very difficult visit emotionally as well as professionally. The man is very abusive and aggressive towards them, in marked contrast to his wife, who is weeping and very distressed. The man actually admits the abuse, but is unable to see that he had done anything wrong.

"She asked for it", he says adamantly; The 'she' in question is 7 years old.

As this case involves forensic (criminal) work, the police have to be involved, which causes further anger from the man, and upsets his wife. Eric finally has to call the police out, when the man starts to attack his wife in front of them.

Paul Lacey (the team Psychiatrist) visits the man in the police cell, and he and Anna will present clinical evidence when their patient finally appears in Court.

By now, it is nearly the end of the working day. Anna decided to go home after this, and relax. A long hot bath, a glass of wine and a good book are her particular needs after a long and tiring day.

Psychotherapists

Theory Training & Methodology
There are many different Schools of Psychotherapy. Its aim is to help clients understand themselves better in order to live more productive lives. Psychotherapy does not tend to take as long as a full Psychoanalysis. 'Psycho' simply means 'of the mind'. Psychotherapy is another 'talking cure'.

The length of training for the Therapists varies greatly, from eighteen month courses for therapists who train in 'brief psychotherapy' to several years. Psychotherapists additionally have to attend for their own therapy, as well as be supervised during their training.

Psychotherapists generally let clients decide what they want to talk about. However, if they feel that clients are evading an issue, or trying to deal with too many areas at one time, they will bring this to their client's attention and re-focus the session on a specific subject.

Type of Client

Generally, clients attending for psychotherapy will have particular problems they want to deal with. Generally, psychotherapy is a very introspective treatment and is not generally used to treat severe and intractable mental illness.

People who have no specific problems, but find life difficult generally difficult to cope with, might benefit from attending psychotherapy sessions, in order to learn more about themselves. Psychotherapy is not often offered to NHS patients in view of the expense involved, and most patients refer privately.

A Day in the Life of a Alison, a Psychotherapist

Alison runs a private practice. She sees each client for about an hour, once a week, and probably for a longish term of about a year. She was a teacher, before deciding in her 40's that she needed a change of direction. Many people do decide quite late in life to train in one of the Therapies, and in fact this is looked upon favourably.

Alison was lucky in that her husband was supportive, and her children in their teenage years, therefore she could invest time, energy, and indeed money, to complete her 2 year training.

Presenting David, from the Case notes of Alison

David has always had difficulties in socializing, although he is an intelligent and attractive man. David finds it difficult to express his feelings when he meets a girl he likes, and after a few dates, he breaks off any budding relationships, then finds himself becoming depressed and angry with himself.

One week, David told Alison about a time his favourite pet dog was run over, but David was unable to cry, even though he really wanted to. He and Alison spent their hour talking about other occasions when sad things happened, and David also found himself unable to express his emotions. Towards the end of the hour, David suddenly remembered that, as a child, he had cried when his favourite teddy had accidentally been thrown away in the rubbish. His father had beaten him with a strap, and told him not to be such a baby. Remembering this in the session with Alison, David began to cry copiously; in fact, he cried for ½ hour unchecked. Alison gently asked him why he was crying, and David said it was the first time he could remember not being punished for crying. They were able to talk about feelings, and how wrong his father was not to have let David express his only too human emotions.

This is an example of a psychotherapy session. A good Psychotherapist, Alison would only see about 4 or 5 patients in a day, as this type of work is very demanding emotionally. Supervision of her work, and writing case notes, would take up a good deal of time, as would the ongoing training which is necessary for all therapists.

Alison likes to be with her family in her free time. She loves her home, and prefers time there to holidays away.

Mental Health Rehabilitation Workers

Theory Training & Methodology
'Rehabilitation Therapists' are paid on unqualified Social Workers scales, and have no qualification they can take in order to improve their salary scales. They are well known in the USA but less well known in the UK. Currently, an NVQ level 3 is being devised in Rehabilitation.

'Rehabs' are a part of the Mental Health Team, and gather up the cases which do not readily fall into the other disciplines. They can act as Social Work Assistants, or train in a particular discipline such as Counselling under their own steam.

Their work is more flexible in that there is no 'formal' entry training, although in effect the 'Rehabs.' are chosen for their maturity, common sense and life experience. They receive on-the-job training in mental health issues and are generally offered other training if they show willingness and aptitude.

Type of Client

Mostly, their caseload consists of patients with long-term mental illnesses, who require Social Skills Training. They might also be allocated shorter-term outpatients, with a variety of needs, from mentoring/counselling, to assisting the Psychologists with people who require behavioural therapy. A Rehabilitation Worker's role could be viewed as an educational one. Generally their caseload would consist of clients with long term and chronic mental illnesses, although they might receive team referrals for clients with short-term problems.

They use a good deal of judgment, both to determine what their clients need, and how to achieve that end in a friendly, relevant and acceptable way. They work with clients to prevent them becoming more ill, and to try to improve their everyday lives.

A Day in the Life of Marlene, Rehabilitation Worker

Marlene has a patient called Yvonne, who has a long-term depressive illness. Marlene visits Yvonne weekly, and takes her shopping. Marlene has devised a long-term programme, which is designed to build Yvonne's confidence in living a normal life, part of which consists of the shopping trips. Marlene suspects that Yvonne is gradually developing agoraphobia, and wants to prevent this happening.

She has arranged to visit Yvonne at 11.00am, and uses the two hours before this first visit of the day to catch up on some housing applications she has made, on behalf of two of Eric's patients. She rings the Housing Office, and discovers that further information is required before the forms can be handed in. Luckily, she has time to quickly visit the Housing Officer, ringing the two applicants for the necessary information.

Today, Yvonne is feeling a little better, and is anxious about the state of her home, which has become untidy whilst she was suffering a bout of depression. Marlene helps her to clear up; this is not strictly part of her job, but she considers it 'practical rehabilitation' for her client, who will benefit psychologically from the better environment.

Afterwards, they devise a written plan. Yvonne is to carry out small amounts of clearing each day, and also to deal regularly with the letters which would otherwise let pile up. Depressive illness takes up a large amount of physical energy. What would normally be simple tasks can become overwhelming during bouts of low mood.

Marlene's second client is Rob, who has recently been bereaved. He just needs to talk, and be reassured. Marlene has arranged for him to be seen by a bereavement Counsellor, who will see him twice a week during the very difficult times of early loss. Rob cries a good deal during Marlene's visit, and talks in detail about Jen's death.

Marlene is herself training in Counselling, but feels she cannot counsel Rob as she has only recently been bereaved herself. Mental health workers have to be very aware of their own limitations at particular times in their lives.

After seeing Rob, Marlene visits Sal, a teenager with schizophrenia who lives in a bedsit, about two miles from her parents home. Sal's parents are very supportive, but are concerned that she visits them three times every day, and is still far too dependent on them. She also wakes them up very early in the morning by banging on the door. Sal is a very pleasant girl, whose delusions are fantastical rather than frightening (she sees and hears Angels), but she is lonely and has poor self care skills.

Today, Marlene is helping Sal to make out a shopping list, to plan what she is going to eat for the week. An O.T. in training had made out a food plan, but it proved far too complex for Sal, who only had a limited attention span, so Marlene decided to simplify it. Sal liked to live on convenience foods, and they planned ready-made pizza, ready prepared salads, baked beans and fruit.

Marlene's next appointment was with Richard, a senior Executive at a local Electronics Company, who had recently become very stressed through overwork. Richard was very wary of being referred by his G.P. to the Community Mental Health Team; initially thought they only saw "mad" people. When the G.P. explained that he could be visited at home, he agreed.

Marlene introduced herself to Richard, and explained the role of the team in Community Mental Health. She then asked him to explain what had happened. After listening, Marlene explained to Richard that 'stress' was an integral part of living, but that excessive stress could build up and affect physical health – even result in heart attacks. She explained the symptoms of stress in detail, and showed him how his inability to remember, and tendency to 'lose' vital documents were quite usual in this situation. Richard was relieved, as he had feared he was "going mad". By now it was 5.30pm, and Marlene had finished her allotted visits for the day. She wrote up her case notes for the Team Meeting on the following morning before leaving the office for home.

Social Workers

Theory Training & Methodology
Social Work trainees have to be at least 22 years of age, with some experience of either working in the field, or voluntary work.

They have to be mature people with some life experience; this is why the age limit is set higher than for training in most professions.

A degree in Social Work takes three years; the trainee then has a degree (Dip SW) in Social Work.

Training is given in Social Policy, Welfare and Legal aspects of the work, with optional training in subjects such as Addictions, Counselling, Psychology, philosophy or learning disability. Social Worker trainees spend a proportion of their training time working on-the-job.

Type of Client
Social Workers do just what their title suggests; they work in social settings, and assist their clients with problems of day-to-day living. They might see people with housing, benefits, neighbour disputes, or difficult behavioural problems.

Social Workers make the applications for detaining people under the Mental Health Act, when people are considered a 'danger to either themselves or the public'.

Many of the people on their caseloads will be 'permanent patients', some with long term mental illnesses (schizophrenia, manic depression). They might also see people with short term difficulties, referred via the Primary Care Team.

A Day in the Life of Eric, a Social Worker
Eric's first appointment of the week is to visit Susie, who is about to divorce, and needs some social support and some financial advice. A court case is pending regarding the sale of the marital home. Susie is meanwhile living with her small daughter in bed and breakfast emergency housing, which Eric helped her find.

Today, he helps Susie to complete Housing Benefit forms, and to look at the possibility of some part time work. Susie is stressed, as this whole situation is unfamiliar to her and she is really worried about the future for herself and her daughter. Just before he leaves, Eric teaches Susie some relaxation techniques and leaves a music tape, which he made for her the previous evening.

Eric has a couple of free hours now, so he returns to his base in the Team office to spend some time writing up his case notes. He also talks to Marlene the Rehab to check up on progress of his patients' housing benefit applications. A welcome cup of coffee with two of his colleagues is followed by a visit to Sam, one of his longer-term patients.

Eric visits Sam to administer a 'depot' injection, which stays in Sam's blood system for about a month, ensuring he stays sane and reasonably able to cope with life in his bedsit. Every week after the injection, Sam attends a day centre. Eric always waits with Sam until the transport bus arrives. They talk about Sam's progress in the week, while Eric monitors Sam's mental state. Sam's conversation reveals how strong or weak his delusions currently are. They also chat about their shared hobby of modelling, and Sam shows him his latest project, a model lunar lander.

When the bus arrives, Eric leaves Eric's house to visit his next patient, Monica. He parks near a field to eat his packed lunch; today he has no time to return to his base.

Monica is not answering her door and Eric is concerned. He knows she is in, as he saw her rushing upstairs as he rang the bell. Eric knows that Monica has not been well for several weeks. She has a diagnosis of schizophrenia, but has refused depot injections.

Eric believes that she has not been taking her medication, and is sure that she needs to be in hospital for a new mental health assessment.

Her neighbour looks up from gardening and recognizes Eric. She tells Eric that Monica has been running around her flat late at night shouting. She believes that her neighbour has not eaten since the weekend. Monica has also broken an upstairs window.

Eric decides that he needs to apply for a sectioning under the Mental Health Act, and calls Dr. Lacey on his mobile phone to discuss his concerns. He drives back to base, and a few hours later has the papers he needs. He returns to the flat with a Police Officer, who has a warrant for forced entry.

After the Police Officer has broken in, Eric finds Monica shivering in her bedroom. She has soiled her clothing, and the flat is in a filthy state. Eric takes the frightened Monica to the hospital in his car, and the neighbour arranges to have the flat boarded up. An hour later, Monica is receiving a visit from Dr Lacey, and has been given injections to make her sleep.

Eric is by now too late for his next two appointments, and telephones to re-make them for the following week. Such juggling of the diary is necessary quite regularly, as each day can bring very different needs.

His last appointment of the day, at 6.30pm, is to help Matt complete his benefit forms. Eric is quite thankful that this will be a straight forward visit. He and Matt complete the forms and eat a plateful of biscuits.

Eric and his partner Sally decide to go to a late night movie. It has been a busy day for them both and a good film will take their minds off work for a few hours.

Hypnotherapists & Hypno Psychotherapists

Theory Training & Methodology

Hypnotherapist and Hypno-psychotherapists are to be found in private practice. The medical profession have not entirely accepted these therapists, and they are considered 'fringe'. Gradually this is changing, just as the professions of chiropractic and osteopathy are now being taken under the wing of mainstream healthcare.

Training for Hypnotherapy or Hypno-Psychotherapy is well over 140 hours, not including on-going professional development. The courses are generally geared towards mental health professionals or mature adults, with a minimum age of 18 years.

Hypnotherapy (the application of hypnosis within the framework of therapy) and Psycho-hypnotherapy (using many different methods of visual imagery and other 'tools' of change) are valuable therapies, dealing with a variety of specific life problems.

The therapists begin with taking a case history, and discuss the nature of the problem with the client. Hypnotherapists will often concentrate on one specific area at a time. 'Hypnotherapy' is a misnomer in that hypnosis is only a small part of what the therapist actually does. He or she will use a variety of methods to help their client resolve problems. It is not simply a matter of 'putting the patient to sleep' and resolving all their problems, as some therapists wrongly believe! 'Brief therapy' is perhaps a better term for this particular way of working.

In hypnosis, the therapist will take particular note of the style of language the client uses, that is whether it is 'visual', 'feeling' or 'auditory' in nature, and will incorporate similar language when the patient is being relaxed for the 'suggestion' or hypnotic part of the therapy.

Clients are encouraged to use vivid imagery to describe the problem, and the therapist makes use of these images as a powerful tool to elicit change in their clients. Refer to the case history below for an example of this method of working.

Type of Client
These therapies are not used for severe mental illness but are very beneficial for phobias, stopping smoking, social or relationship problems, and problems of a general nature.

A series of sessions with a 'brief therapist' (the term I prefer to use) might be from 4 to 20, or perhaps a little longer. Some therapists claim to treat disorders in far shorter a time, but naturally this depends on the client and on what they are bringing to the session.

Case History from a Hypno-Psychotherapist
Jason was a banker, who in his spare time liked to devote himself to Community work. He had already taken training with CRUSE (who provide bereavement counselling) and RELATE (dealing with relationships), but felt he needed to move into the area of brief, time limited therapy. His aim was to build up a private practice, and earn his living in a way which more suited the person he felt he wanted to become.

Nearly 18 months later, and Jason was able to start his own private practice. His supervisor is Mandy, a therapist who has been working for many years in her own practice. He sees her once a week, for about 2 hours, depending upon how many clients he is seeing.

First through the door this morning is Andy, who has facial twitches. These are uncommon, and very distressing. People can be very cruel, and Andy has been teased about 'winking' on numerous occasions, not only by children, but also by adults.

Jason takes a case history first of all, and asks Andy about the nature of the twitches, sometimes referred to as 'tics'. When Andy relates the large number of 'tics', and also the fact that he gets very angry easily, Jason starts to consider that Andy might need a different kind of treatment than the one he can offer. He suspects that Andy does not have a simple tic, but a form of 'Tourettes' disorder, which is more serious, and needs psychiatric treatment.

Andy is naturally upset; he thought a few sessions of hypnosis would be enough for him. In common with many other people, he is afraid of Psychiatrists. However, Jason persuades him that medication might be very effective, and help with his mood problems as well. He offers to refer him via a colleague he met at his training school, and finally Andy agrees. Jason will lose a client, but he would rather do this, and see the person obtain the right treatment.

Jason's next client is Daisy, who is about to go on holiday, but is afraid of flying. She has booked the holiday in a desperate attempt to overcome her illness, as she feels her family are also suffering from their constant UK holidays. Jason will have to work fast, as the holiday is only three weeks away.

He takes a case history, and finds out that her phobia ('fear') occurred after a traumatic flight three years' ago, when turbulence caused her plane to crash land on the runway. Unfortunately, on the next flight she took, a man tried to hijack the plane, although luckily without success. Since then, Daisy had been afraid of going any where near aeroplanes.

Jason spent some time reassuring the woman that these incidents, although occurring within a short time frame, were highly unusual, and unlikely to occur again. They discussed her reactions to the situations. Finally, Jason induced a hypnotic state (trance or very deep relaxation), and allowed her to 'imagine' the events happening again. First of all, she was to imagine the events as they were. Whilst doing this, Jason noted her breathing rate rapidly increasing and her fists clenching.

In the second 'trance', she had to imagine the same events but concentrate on her breathing, rather than the events around her. Jason noticed that she used very visual words like "seeing this happen" and "I saw red". He used similar imagery to appeal to her unconscious mind, and more easily relax her into a trance state. This method is, if you like, rather like wearing the same 'psychological clothing' as the client. This works because we all respond better to those who appear to be similar to ourselves in some way.

The trance state took a while for Daisy to get used to, but by the end of the hour-long session, she was feeling better. Jason decided to see her twice more after that, each time encouraging her to concentrate on her breathing and hand movements.

In the event, Daisy was able to get on the aeroplane, albeit still feeling nervous. There was a little turbulence, but she managed to put herself into a trance state, and coped with it. Several years later, and Daisy is still happily boarding planes with her family.

Jason had four other appointments that day, after which he was ready for his nightly treat of a long telephone chat with his friend Suzanne, and a few hours surfing the Internet.

Summary Of Section

A "Therapy" is 'a curative medical treatment'. A 'Therapist' is one who gives out treatment.

- People who choose to go privately can choose to whom they go. If a patient is referred to a Community Mental Health Team, that decision is made for them.
- All therapists have their own theories as to what causes their patients or clients to have life difficulties.
- The best therapists have experienced their own often traumatic life problems, and overcome them.
- All good therapists have Supervision and undergo their own therapy.
- Choose a Therapist by asking yourself; when I talk, do I feel they understand me?

The Therapists

Counsellors are qualified Therapists who use 'talking cures' to relieve their clients problems

General Practitioners are Doctors trained in medicine. "Doctor" refers to their Degree, or Doctorate. They are legally responsible for the clinical welfare of their patients

Registered Mental Nurses are trained to diagnose and treat with therapy the major mental illnesses. They administer drugs, which have to be prescribed by Psychiatrists or General Practitioners.

Occupational Therapists are specialists in assessing physical disability. In Mental Health, they assess for disability aids (e.g. chair hoists), occupations, and disability benefits

Pharmacists are highly qualified chemists (scientists). They have more knowledge of drugs than GPs, although currently the law does not allow them to prescribe, only dispense

A Psychiatrist is a qualified Medical Doctor, with psychiatric training. He prescribes drugs which will have a positive effect on the brain chemistry of his mentally ill patients.

A Psycho-Analyst is a person who helps his patients to understand themselves, by analysing their everyday reactions to people and situations in life.

Clinical Psychologists have a deep understanding of human behaviour (why people do certain things) and use this knowledge to help their patient understand their problems and resolve them

Psychotherapy is another word for 'therapy of the mind'. Similar to Psychologists, Psychotherapists help their patients to understand themselves and their lives

'Rehabs' are a part of the Mental Health Team, and offer mentoring and social skills training for long term mentally ill

Social Workers work in social settings, and aim to make better the practical conditions under which their patients live. They deal with 'sectioning', housing, benefits, social problems

Hypnotherapists and Hypno-psychotherapists work privately, as this particular profession has not yet been accepted by the mainstream medical people

"Arsonist .. who has served 21 years in jail, is on the move today. The man who put him behind bars, Judge…. wrote "In a just Society, he should not be in prison at all, but in a secure place where he could receive treatment"

Local newspaper report

CHAPTER 7

Therapeutic Communities And Hospitals

This Chapter includes:
Asylums
Psychiatric Hospitals
Self Help and Support Groups
Therapeutic Communities

Asylum – a 'Place of Refuge'

Bethlem Asylum was set up in 1377, funded by public subscriptions. 'Asylum' meant 'a place of refuge'. It was on the site of a much earlier Priory, the Church of St Mary of Bethlehem, after which it was named. In 1403 the inhabitants included poor and physically ill patients as well as the mentally ill. In effect, Asylums became dumping grounds for unwanted relatives and 'misfits'.

Private 'madhouses' also existed at this time, run as businesses. Wealthy patients paid for their keep; poor people had their accommodation paid by the Parish. It was common for the insane to be prosecuted and imprisoned for bizarre or anti-social manner, and Bethlem became an alternative to prison.

Early 'Care' of the Insane

Although mental illness was not recognised in the same way as physical illness at this time, there was some acknowledgement that such people needed care. When Bethlem was built, no one who entered was expected to recover; most people would die within the walls.

Patients, both male and female, were kept in appalling conditions, naked, often restrained or chained, with straw for bedding. On Sundays, the public were allowed to pay to 'view' them for entertainment, however, serious visitors were discouraged. In 1770 this disgraceful practice was banned.

Treatment consisted of vomiting and purging to weaken the patients, and therefore lessen any potential violence. It was considered wasteful to give out too much food, in view of the nature of the "treatment". The Doctors in this establishment formulated their own medicines, with none of the clinical trials which exist today. The patients were forced to pay for these drugs, so the Doctors made handsome profits.

If a patient was discharged, he/she was given a badge, which was a license to beg in the surrounding villages. They then had to pay back the costs of the treatment they had received in Bethlem out of the proceeds of this 'work'.

Victorian Asylums

Many of the Victorian Asylums held as many as 900 patients. These Asylums were very large buildings, self-contained Communities with their own kitchens, chapels and workshops. The grounds were spacious, and each would have its kitchen garden.

Patients worked within the Asylum, either at some trade, or perhaps in the kitchen gardens. Treatments began to improve, and mental illness began to be regarded as separate from criminality.

The 1960's

Even beyond Victorian times, Asylums were being used as dumping places for 'mental defectives'. Only a few years ago I met some of the last surviving patients who suffered this cruel method of social injustice. In their late 80's/90's, they had lived out their lives in Asylums, with no-where else to go.

One patient was an unmarried mother who had been branded 'a social misfit'; another had stolen a bicycle when he was a teenager and had been 'put away' by his embarrassed parents. Yet another, somewhat of a 'mummy's boy', had been unable to cope with life when his mother died, and eventually ended up in an Asylum because there was nowhere else for him to go.

Despite the grim Victorian buildings still being used, many and varied facilities were set up in the Asylums (now being revamped as 'Psychiatric Hospitals'), such as libraries, shops, Occupational Therapy units, a patient's canteen and a large laundry. In effect, it provided Community living, and a real place of refuge, for staff as well as patients. The Asylums usually had their own chapel and Chaplain.

I remember the Asylum where I worked in the 1960's had a patient who frequently harangued the Minister in his pulpit, to the amusement of the whole congregation. The lady was tolerated, as her behaviour was recognised to be a part of her illness.

Visits to the town for coffee and walks were frequent, and considered part of the treatment. The residents of the local village seemed tolerant of the patients, having being used to many years of the bizarre antics which some of the patients exhibited, this being long before anti psychotic drugs which controlled the excesses of such behaviour.

There were dances and visits out as 'treats' for the patients, and in many ways the Asylum performed the role of a home. Some of the wards were locked, not because of potential patient violence, but because patients tended to wander off when unsupervised.

Care in the Community– the 1990's

Loneliness – *I once saw a man from one of the local Group Homes for the recovering mentally ill, standing on a street corner. As I was driving past, I saw that he was singing to himself, and cradling in his* *arms a pile of incontinence pads, held close like a baby. His face expressed incredible sadness.*

Quite a proportion of the patients did not want to leave their Asylum home, where they had friends and activities, and felt secure. Although it appeared that the Community was tolerant with patients when they returned each evening to their Asylum, it was a different matter when the Government decided that everyone must live in the same Community.

Some patients went to live in communal or 'group' homes, which were houses purchased privately in residential areas. Each of these homes would receive one or two visits a week from mental health workers, more for severely ill patients. Three or four ex in-patients might live together under one roof; compatibility being a matter of good judgement or luck or the right medication.

Some patients were given Council bedsits or flats, and were left to their own devices for most of the week, seeing only their Social Service visitors perhaps once or twice a week. I have seen a fair amount of loneliness in these circumstances. Those people with severe mental illness needed space, but were not well equipped to organize their own daily routine, which can be difficult even for those with full mental faculties.

Care in the Community was based on the premise that the Community itself cares. In fact, public reaction might range from tolerance, through indifference, to outright hostility.

I know of one instance where a so-called 'sane' person threatened to shoot the patients who were about to be housed in a pleasant area, next door to him. The authorities unfortunately bowed to this threat, and the patients had to be housed elsewhere. A vital ingredient had been left out; that of 'educating' and reassuring the community about their new neighbours. A lack of facilities to treat those few mentally ill patients who were potentially violent, and little legal backup to ensure they could be treated compulsorily if necessary, added to the problem. The result was a whole raft of negative press articles and prisons crammed to overflowing with untreated ex-psychiatric patients.

Many of the former Asylums, with poorly decorated wards and inefficient heating systems, have been closed and converted to luxury homes. It is ironic that the wealthier of the Community are now enjoying these homes, whilst the mentally ill live in 'social housing', or overcrowded prisons.

Psychiatric Hospitals

An average Psychiatric Hospital in the 1990's might have one or two permanent wards, a large outpatients department for day cases, and teaching facilities for junior Psychiatric staff. Rooms would be available for the therapists to see their out-patient's. There are specialized services, such as Art therapy, group therapy, and perhaps generalized classes on subjects such as assertion training, as well as meeting spaces for groups such as Alcoholics Anonymous, or Mind.

Some of the day patients do not like sitting in the Reception of a Psychiatric Hospital, where they come into contact with patients with severe mental illnesses. NHS mental health departments still lack the resources to provide more congenial settings.

Self Help Or Support Groups

There are many support groups, variable in both type and content. The fact that you share a diagnosis does not necessarily mean that you will like either the folk in your group, or even the format the meetings take. However, they do fill a gap, and I know that many users find them invaluable, especially on those long, lonely Bank Holiday weekends.

There are now many supportive groups in the UK for those with access to the Internet (and you can find computers at main libraries too), and can even key into the millions of groups in the USA. You will find everything, from herpes to bereavement to GP's who will answer health queries by email.

The Samaritans

Founded in 1953 by Chad Varah, an Anglican vicar who wanted to find a way of alleviating the suffering of the suicidal, this voluntary organisation now has over 200 branches nation-wide, and over 20,000 volunteers. They offer year round, 24 hour listening to fellow human beings who have reached the depths of despair, and need an objective, but sympathetic and non-judgmental listening ear.

Volunteers from all walks of life undergo a selection process, followed by about 30 hours of training, and six months probationary period. These people are specially selected for their life experience and ability; they also are well supervised and supported.

Samaritans went 'online' in 1994, offering a confidential email service to their users, in addition to the usual telephone lines. Contact details are in the Web and Book recommendations in the last chapter of this book.

Living in a Therapeutic Community

Question: "What is the difference between a Therapist and a patient, in a therapeutic community?
Answer: "The patients get better and go home."

An amusing way of illustrating the lack of boundaries between therapists and patients in a therapeutic community. Relaxed living is the usual style.

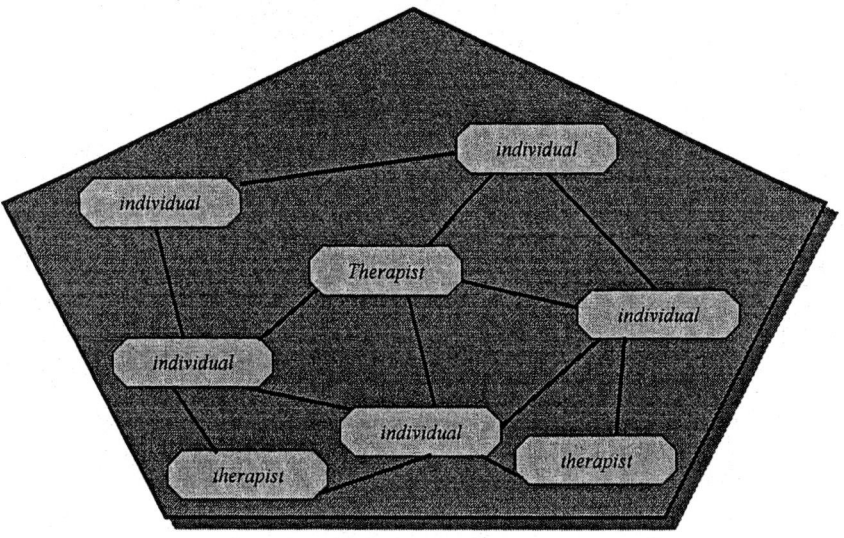

I have attempted to show, in this schematic diagram, the informal relationships between the therapists and patients, in a therapeutic community. All learn from each other.

Potential positive aspects of this type of therapy
- Man is a social animal - community living is therefore 'normal'
- a person will be more self aware in a supportive group
- more security exists - both physical and mentally

Potential negative aspects
- A group can destroy individuals, without taking responsibility individually
- A person will develop differently in a group, than he/she will when alone
- individuals and therapists can become 'institutionalised'
  i.e. unable to live outside the community

Therapeutic Communities

An uncommon form of treatment, 'Therapeutic Communities' consist of therapists and patients living together in a communal building. The Community is a self-functioning and self governing group, existing to deal with such long term difficulties as addictions, behavioural problems, personality disorders, and emotional disorders.

Patients are encouraged to take part in the management of the Community, and the many weekly meetings to discuss areas of difficulty or progress. There are drawbacks to Therapeutic Communities. They can become potential hot beds for the exchanging of illnesses, as well as giving potential for real growth for personalities.

Each day is very structured, and consists of a number of therapeutic activities, interspersed with 'chores' such as gardening, cleaning, and DIY projects. The therapies can range widely, and include some which are not offered by mainstream medical people, for example:

- art therapy
- psychodrama
- gardening therapy

Group therapy, women's and men's groups, and group psychotherapy are also available, designed to encourage eventual integration back into the community. Within the group, participants learn to express themselves in different ways, receiving the positive or negative feedback from both other members of the group and from the staff, which promotes further self awareness.

An example of such a Community is HMP Grendon Underwood in Buckinghamshire, opened in 1962 "as an experimental psychiatric prison to provide treatment for prisoners with antisocial personality disorders".

There are 5 therapeutic communities within the prison, each operating separately. Prisoners choose to serve their sentence at Grendon, and must agree to stay for at least 2 years of their sentence. They must be committed to stay drug free and to have a 'genuine desire for change'. It is not an easy option, but there has been a high degree of success; two Butler national prison awards have been won for the work being carried out with prisoners at Grendon.

Summary Of Section

Asylums
- An "Asylum" is 'a place of refuge'. Up to the 1980's, many of the Victorian Asylums held as many as 900 patients.
- Communal or 'group' homes, are houses or blocks of flats, where people with long term mental illness live within the community. Some people live in Social Housing, seeing Social Service visitors perhaps once a week.
- An average Psychiatric Hospital in the 1990's might have one or two permanent wards, a large outpatients department (for day cases) and teaching facilities for junior Psychiatric staff.

Self Help Or Support Groups
'Samaritans' was founded in 1953 by Chad Varah, an Anglican vicar who wanted to find a way of alleviating the suffering of the suicidal. This voluntary organisation now has over 200 branches nation-wide, and over 20,000 volunteers, providing year round, 24 hour listening to fellow human beings who have reached the lowest levels of despair.

Asylums, Psychiatric Hospitals, Therapeutic Communities, Self Help and Support Groups are also 'therapies', based on the treatment of patients as groups as well as individuals.

Therapeutic Communities
Set up with long term therapy of behavioural, emotional and addictive problems in mind. Useful in the exchange of ideas and responsibilities and potential growth factors. Negative aspects; learning new 'negative' behaviours, losing identity, difficulty of finding individuality in a group.

I want you to remember; a case history represents a person, and we should be full of awe for those who not only survive these emotionally crippling illnesses, but learn from them.

Marianne

Chapter 8

Case Histories

This chapter includes:
A useful exercise in diagnosis from a case history
Descriptions of the following major mental illnesses:
- Brief Psychotic Disorder
- Depressive Illness
- Eating Disorders
- Mania
- Obsessive Compulsive Disorder
- Personality Disorders – some of the many types
- Phobias
- Schizophrenia

Each disorder described in the following pattern
- a brief description of the illness
- a list of symptoms - mental and physical
- causes, with an indication of recurrence in % of the population
- known cures or effective remedies
- case history

In this section, I would like to look at how the medical profession diagnose and treat major mental illnesses. The following are some of the most commonly known illnesses. I have tried to enliven each of these with a brief Case History.

A Useful Exercise in Diagnosis from a Case History

For each of the Sectional notes on the specific illnesses, note the bullets I have marked against the symptoms, causes, and cures. At various points in each case history, I have marked with corresponding bullets the areas where a professional might note from the 'case history' as symptoms, causes, or potential cures for the patient's specific illness. Look out for these symbols: ■, ◆, ➢, which I have used to represent;

■ symptom ◆cause ➢cure

in the corresponding Sectional notes. I have written this exercise to give the reader some understanding of how a professional would diagnose during the taking of a case history. Remember, that each person's experience of these disorders is different, even within one particular diagnostic category.

A Personal View

When I was writing this book, I came to the conclusion that nothing I had met in the world of mental illness was different to everyday experience, except in extremes of behaviour or degree of severity. I am not asking you to accept major mental illnesses as 'normal', but to consider the roots of these illnesses within the 'normal' functioning human mind.

It is only by considering mental illness to be a human process gone awry, that those who suffer such devastating illnesses can be viewed as fellow human beings, rather than creatures apart. Such humanistic views are vital to further both tolerance and the very real need to urge public pressure for securing more funding. Research, treatment, places of refuge, and (vitally) more trained therapists in the field of mental illness are desperately required at a greater level than at present funded by the Government.

When you read the case histories I present, please remember remind yourself "there, but for grace, go I"; for mental illness can strike any one of us at any time; all social levels, all races. At some time in the future, I hope to present a book about my own experience of mental illness. I do not write merely from clinical knowledge, but from personal and painful life experience.

I too have had to 'learn' my understanding and tolerance. Follow me then with wonder and admiration for those who undergo the extreme challenge of recovering from these terrible illnesses.

Description of Brief Psychotic Disorder

Brief Psychotic Disorder is a medical term, which lay people sometimes refer to as "nervous breakdown". The latter describes the condition quite well; literally, an illness lasting only a short time, during which the patient's nervous system exhibits the symptoms of a 'psychosis'. A 'psychosis' is used to describe symptoms which result in the patient losing temporary touch with the everyday world; disorganized speech, delusions, and hallucinations, which alter the perception of reality.

A Psychosis can be considered as a 'fragmenting' of the mind, usually of brief duration. During this very frightening experience, the everyday world takes on the aspects of a nightmare. Imagine a terrifyingly real nightmare which lasts throughout the day and into the night.

Sleep is fitful, and the 'out of touch with reality' experience so real, that, waking either very early or very late, it is impossible for the sufferer to work out whether it is daytime or night-time. Look at some of the classical art works in the Galleries, where 'day into night' features as a theme of some artists. The day may be filled with hallucinations, and feelings of paranoia (fear of a specific thing or person) quickly develop. Disembodied voices may be heard, threatening the person with death or annihilation. Daily life becomes extremely difficult, sometimes impossible.

Trust rapidly disappears. The symptoms are strongly reminiscent of those experienced by people with a schizophrenic illness, or as a result of taking drugs and having a bad 'trip'.

Symptoms:

Physical
- Speech is not clear
- Symptoms of 'withdrawal', similar to catatonic schizophrenia
- Disheveled appearance

Mental
- Hallucinations – i.e. patient sees or hears things that are not there
- Inability to concentrate
- Extreme fear
- Confusion about time orientation
- Delusions –strong fixed ideas or beliefs which untrue in reality

Causes

Generally attributed to one or more of the following:
- ♦ Any major life stress
- ♦ Following the trauma of childbirth

This disorder is uncommon.

Cures/ Remedies

- ➤ Medications which change the brain chemistry
- ➤ Possible detainment in a Psychiatric Hospital
- ➤ Supportive counselling
- ➤ Given time, the brief psychosis will heal itself

DEVELOPMENT OF A BRIEF PSYCHOSIS

Major life catastrophe

Worry causes sleeplessness
fear causes further sleeplessness

Lack of concentration

Other events 'pile in'

Extreme fear develops

Sleeplessness leads to hallucinations

Person starts to withdraw

Delusions set in: triggered
by the hallucinations

Medication reduces Psychotic symptoms

Later, Counselling explores life history & helps
prevent re-occurrence through self knowledge

Delusions: fears not based on reality

Hallucination: seeing things that others do not

Psychotic: extreme fear, based on
poor perceptions of reality

Look out for the corresponding bullets in the description of the illness ■ ◆ ➢

Case History – Brief Psychosis

Jane

"If I knew that I had to go through a similar experience again, I would kill myself right now. It was like hell. I really thought that 'they' were following me, and trying to control my mind. Everyone was in the plot, even my Doctor and my husband. I felt I could trust no one. It was like being in a nightmare, only the nightmare went on during the day as well. I could not 'wake up'. Imagine a nightmare that goes on for weeks; it is enough to drive you insane. If I had not gone into hospital, then I am sure I would have never recovered."

Jane is 40, and has recently separated after many years of marriage. Neither the marriage nor Jane's childhood were happy experiences ◆. She has no living family, lives a solitary existence, and has a mundane clerical job which is far below her capability.

Joe, one of her friends, had noticed that Jane had left her answer phone on for over two weeks, and had not replied to his calls. Although it was customary for Jane not to answer every call, this length of time was unusual ■. When he called at her flat soon after work one evening, the curtains were closed, and he noticed an upstairs light on, even though it was light outside ■.

Joe did not receive a reply to his call, and he rang Cynthia, another mutual friend. Cynthia said that Jane had not attended their writing group for two weeks, which was unusual ■, as this was Jane's only outing during the week. Next morning, Joe and Cynthia called Jane's employer, who said she had been acting oddly over the past few weeks, seeming to be withdrawing into herself at work ■. Her work had not been up to the usual standard ■. The Personnel Officer had called to the house several times without success.

Joe and Cynthia called the Police, and relayed their concerns to them. A warrant was obtained for them to enter Jane's house.

A Police Officer and Social Worker met Joe and Cynthia at the house. After ringing the bell for some time, Jane answered the door. Her two friends were shocked by her appearance, which was wild and disheveled ■. Jane looked terrified. She refused to allow the Police Officer in, but the other three were allowed entry.

The house was in a mess with litter and half eaten meals in every room. Cynthia tried to hug Jane, but Jane backed off, and crouched in her chair, shouting every few minutes to someone she could obviously see ■, but no one else in the room could.

The Social Worker asked Jane many questions. Jane eventually revealed that she had been to see her General practitioner a few days previously, but that she had had to rush out, as a man in the Surgery Waiting Room was listening to everything she was telling her GP ■, and making notes. All this seemed very real to Jane ■.

The Social Worker took Joe and Cynthia aside, and said Jane would have to be detained under the Mental Health Act, and taken to a Psychiatric Hospital for treatment. Joe asked if he and Cynthia could take her, as he was aware that, were Jane to be committed ("Sectioned" ➤), then it would not look good on her employment record. The Social Worker agreed.

After about an hour of gentle coaxing, Jane was finally persuaded to go to Hospital with her friends. She was admitted later that evening, and Cynthia was allowed to stay quite late in her dormitory.

When the Consultant Psychiatrist arrived, Jane began to show signs of fear again. Some medication ➤was prescribed and a Mental Nurse on the Ward gave Jane the tablet, which she refused. Cynthia asked the Nurse to leave them for a while, then asked Jane why she was not taking the medication, which would help her. Jane said, that she feared the Psychiatrist was trying to poison her ■. Jane's belief about this was so strong that Cynthia could not persuade her otherwise.

Eventually, the Nurse returned, and quickly injected Jane with a drug which soon calmed her, and put her to sleep.

Cynthia and Joe visited Jane regularly over the next few weeks, and gradually noticed she was improving. They were told by the Mental Nurse that Jane was receiving Counselling➤, as well as the medication ➤. The Counsellor was talking to Jane about her life, and the turmoil of events which may have lead up to her psychosis. Jane had been terrified by her ordeal ■, and found it difficult to talk at first, but gradually built up a trusting relationship with the Counsellor.

Several weeks after entering Hospital, Jane was discharged, and continued her Counselling ➤ sessions at home. By now, she was embarrassed by what had happened, and could even wryly smile at the thought that the Consultant had been trying to poison her; the thought had been very real at the time.

Almost a year later, Jane found the confidence to find a more demanding job ➤ and, supported by Joe, Cynthia and her other friends, began to build a new life for herself. The symptoms of the psychosis did not return.

Depressive Illness

Severe depressive illness can be lethal. People of all ages and all different walks of life do take their own lives. Depressive illness is surprisingly common; about 1 in 4 may be treated for it at some time during their lives. It is often mis-used as a term to describe any kind of life sadness, but this in no way conveys the depth of suffering and the length of time over which the condition lasts.

The adjective 'depressed' is often wrongly used to describe sadness e.g. "I was really depressed", meaning, 'I was very sad'. The difference between sadness and depression is like the difference between a mild cold and pneumonia.

Suicidal Urges

Almost inevitable with a very severe depression, suicidal urges are very strong. It is only the person's physical inability to do anything that prevents suicide in the deepest depths of the illness, although plans for dying are often made during this time. It seems to be Nature's way of saying 'think about this'. People commit suicide as they are recovering their energy, and have the physical strength to carry out their plan. No one knows what occurs in those fateful minutes after the final decision has been made.

There has been much controversy over a book about self-deliverance, written by a Doctor, which details precisely how suicide can be carried out successfully. I read this book, and found it written in a sincere fashion. Part of the book is devoted to asking the reader if they are sure this is the only way out; part easing the pain of loss for relatives and friends. The Doctor (Derek Humphry) assisted his wife to commit suicide, when she was suffering a terminal illness. Indeed, this is the only occasion for which he advocates the use of suicide; to cure unrelenting pain. His point in writing, was to save the unnecessary suffering of a bungled suicide attempt.

Symptoms list:
At least 5 of the following must be present almost every day:

Physical
- Sleep disturbances (lack of, or increase of)
- Lack of energy
- Decrease or increase in physical movements
- Changes to weight and appetite (increase or decrease)
- Withdrawal from activity and social life

Mental
- Persistently low mood (irritability in children and teens.)
- Tearfulness
- Lack of concentration or decisiveness
- Lack of pleasure in everyday life and activity
- Feelings of guilt or worthlessness
- Thoughts or desire of death

Causes:

- devastating life events
- loss e.g. bereavement, amputation, job, opportunity, relationship
- family history of the illness
- isolation
- changes to the brain chemistry
- abuse of alcohol or drugs

What experts do not yet know, is why one person may have any of the above difficulties and yet may not suffer a depressive illness. The reasons may or may not be related to genetic factors. This is a common illness, affecting about 5% of women and 2 –3% of men. Prisoners in solitary confinement, refugees, soldiers under battle conditions, the injured of major accidents, and long married people who have been recently separated people are highly likely to become clinically depressed. It's to do with isolation, severe shock or being in a hostile environment.

Cures/ Remedies

- ➢ Medications which change the brain chemistry
- ➢ Talking cures
- ➢ Electro Convulsive therapy
- ➢ Psychotherapy or counselling
- ➢ Cognitive-Behavioural Therapy

How do Clinicians know that the depression is 'clinical' i.e. severe enough to warrant urgent treatment? They use a testing system such as the 'Beck Depression Inventory'(BDI) (refer to diagram). This is a questionnaire with multiple-choice answers, each of which has a scored rating. The added scores are measured against a scale, which quite accurately scores the severity of the illness. Patients are given this questionnaire periodically, to test the shifting pattern of their illness. I have listed some of the questions in the Becks diagram later in this chapter.

Look out for the corresponding bullets in the description of the illness

Case History – Depressive Illness

Sally
"It was like being at the bottom of a deep pit. No ladder was long enough to reach down and help pull me out. All the time, I felt I had a shadow following me – my 'Black Shadow'. Even at the point that I was sitting comatose in a chair at home, I was aware of friends visiting me. I could not respond, and sometimes I didn't even want them there, but all the time I was saying to myself for God's sake don't leave me alone with myself. It was the most isolating experience I have suffered in my life, and every day I thought about it would be better not to have to wake up each morning."

Sally, had reached her 46th birthday. She was feeling very unhappy, having suffered bouts of depressive illness throughout her life ◆, which had never been treated, although several times she had half-heartedly seen a Counsellor. Sally had never liked to talk about her feelings, and would break off her therapy to avoid feeling uncomfortable. Sally had suffered so long, that she had almost become used to her illness, which she called her "Black Shadow". She was one of many people who give their illness a name, as if it were a tangible object.

Her own mother, who also suffered depressive illness ◆, died age 46, after a very unhappy married life. Sally thought often about her mother. She regarded her mother's life as being wasted on the wrong person, and was also angry at both parents for her own unhappy and isolated childhood ◆. Sally was married to John, a kind man, but he also found it difficult to talk about feelings.

When she became depressed, he would anxiously try to do things for her, rather than talk, but on the whole he found it difficult to understand what was happening to his wife.

Over a period of several months, Sally had become very withdrawn, and so low in mood that John became frightened for her■. If John tried to talk to her, she snapped back, or burst into tears ■. Over several weeks, Sally withdrew more and more. She would sit around for long periods, doing nothing, as the house became dirtier and the washing piled up.

Sally no longer had the energy or inclination ■ to make love with John, and rejected his advances. John also felt rejected, and stopped trying after a few months. He started an affair with a colleague where he worked. He tried to avoid Sally by going out to the pub more often after work, sometimes coming home drunk.

Whereas most people would feel alert after sleeping all night, Sally woke from her restless sleep feeling heavy and tired ■, as if she had had no sleep at all. Most of the night, she had lain awake just thinking, but not productive thinking with a result; this was just repeated thoughts about the inevitable worthlessness of her life ■.

Most of her friends stopped visiting, as they could not cope with seeing her suffering; when they did visit, Sally would just sit in her chair, rarely responding to them.

Eventually, Sally stopped bothering to get up at all. Feeling more and more isolated and lonely, despite all the efforts of her partner, Sally had decided that it would be better to die. She had no energy to carry out her plans, but she spent a lot of time thinking about it. At this point, John took the bull by the horns, and insisted that Sally went with him to their GP ➤.

Sally's G.P. prescribed some anti-depressant medication for her to take, to lift her mood ◆, and at the same time made an appointment for her to see a Psychiatrist at the local Psychiatric Hospital ➤. Both John and Sally were reluctant for her to go to the Hospital; they both felt that only 'mad' people went to those places.

The G.P. was able to reassure them that Psychiatric Hospitals were just specialist places for people with mental health problems, and that she would only be attending as a 'day patient' ➤. John asked anxiously how long Sally's treatment would take. The G.P. was only able to estimate that she would attend for quite a few months; the Psychiatrist would probably see her weekly at first, then monthly.

Sally would also need to see a Psychologist➤ at regular intervals, to help her regain her confidence and her interest in life. The G.P. wanted John to be involved in Sally's treatment as well, and agreed that John could attend some of the appointments with her.

Sally attended as an outpatient for almost a year➢; she and the Psychologist had found that many of her difficulties had started way back in her childhood.

Throughout this period, Sally's recovery was erratic; once or twice, she slipped back into a depression. However, she was now reassured by the staff, and agreed on one occasion to be treated as an in-patient. At the same time, John found the courage to seek some Counselling therapy➢ for himself, and was actually relieved when he started to talk about himself and his feelings – it made things easier at home. He was also given a great deal of information about depressive illness.

As Sally recovered, she and John realized that they needed to separate; they had both become very different people. Although it was a sad decision, they knew it was best for both of them, and they agreed to try to remain in contact. Sally wished that her own mother had taken the decision to divorce, and became sad when she was reminded of past events.

Sally started training for a new job as a Nursery Nurse➢; she had always loved children, but felt she would be unable to cope with being a mother herself. She decided to stay in the family home, to give herself some feelings of security. John visited her, and they were able to talk about themselves for the first time in many years. Sally started to go out and make new friends, although she still found that she liked being in her own home more than going out.

SAMPLE QUESTIONS FROM 'BECK'S DEPRESSION INVENTORY (B.D.I.)

Each question has a score rating - the scores are added for all of the questions
(NB not all the questions, of which there are over 20, are shown here.

For each of the questions, the patient is asked to mark the one answer which most closely matches his/her feelings AT THE TIME OF THE TEST. The test is given periodically through the treatment, to monitor any improvement or regression.

The test can obviously be 'faked'; but this in itself would denote a problem

0 is a low score; 3 is the highest score.

B.D.I.

which answers describe how you feel NOW?
tick one box only for each question

Question 1
0   I do not feel sad ☐
1   I feel sad ☐
2   I am sad all the time, and I can't snap out of it ☐
3   I am so sad or unhappy that I can't stand it ☐

Question 3
0   I do not feel like a failure ☐
1   I feel I have failed more than the average person ☐
2   As I look back on my life, all I can see is a lot of failures ☐
3   I feel I am a complete failure as a person ☐

Question 9
0   I don't have thoughts of killing myself ☐
1   I have thoughts of killing myself, but I wouldn't carry them out ☐
2   I would like to kill myself ☐
3   I would kill myself if I had the chance ☐

The score ratings are added together for all of the questions.

The Clinician looks at the five score ratings, range from normal through to a severe depression,

These tests have been proven to be very accurate in Clinical use.

Eating Disorders

Formerly divided into 'anorexia nervosa' and 'bulimia nervosa', eating disorders are physically and psychologically crippling. Anorexic people tended to restrict their intake of food; people with bulimia tended to binge eat then purge (using laxatives or by vomiting).

Do you remember being a teenager, and thinking you were fat, and perhaps when you were older, perhaps 30 or 40, you looked at the photos and thought, I wasn't fat at all, I was quite normal? It's the same sort of mental trick being played within the minds of people with eating disorders. People find it difficult to understand that teenagers weighing 6 stones or less still consider themselves "fat"; still more shocking that 25%* of those admitted for treatment will die.

Force feeding only helps survival. In order to 'cure' this illness (and it is extremely difficult), the sufferer has to learn to see themselves as 'normal'.

It is not that these patients do not want to eat, for they often crave food, and are obsessed by it. The drive to not eat and to purge are impossible to control. It is a very frightening illness. A stage when the body organs just cannot cope with the lack of nourishment.

Even among medical staff, this illness is misunderstood, and perhaps the eating-disordered do not always receive the sympathetic approach that they need. Families are devastated – imagine what it is like, to see your daughter or son starving to death in front of your eyes, and you can do nothing.

Symptoms list:
Generally, about 2 episodes a week for 3 months of the physical and mental symptoms:

Physical
- Body weight fluctuation
- Recurrent vomiting or purging (induced by patient), or restricting intake of food
- Tooth decay, because of stomach acids deposited from vomiting
- Menstrual cycles disrupted and may disappear altogether

Mental
- fear of gaining weight (anorexia)
- body shape becomes obsessive
- belief that the patient is 'judged' by their appearance

Possible Causes
- media obsession with 'thinness' especially in fashion world
- history of family problems
- fear of growing up and facing independence
- bullying or teasing at school, especially about their appearance
- desire to 'control' themselves, their families
- devastating experiences, such as rape
- family physical or psychological abuse

Occurrence is about 1 –3% of the population.

Cures/ Remedies
- compulsory hospitalization with a strict feeding regime
- psychotherapy
- group therapy
- media and psychiatrists liaising over 'normal' body images

Look out for the corresponding bullets in the description of the illness
■ ◆ ➢

Case History- Eating Disorders
Fay

"It seems hard to believe it now, looking back after nearly 18 months on the ward. I mean, I was literally a walking skeleton. Mum showed me some of the photos they had taken; all I could see was this totally out-of-control fat person. You know what finally turned things for me? It was Janine, my room-mate on the Ward. They said I could say goodbye to her before the undertakers came. There was the bed, and this rumpled sheet on it. I thought that they had already taken her but, I was curious enough to look under the sheet. I couldn't stop vomiting, even though there was nothing to vomit. Suddenly, I couldn't control myself, and I was scared."

Fay walked slowly into the office, saw me, and smiled wanly. Just behind the thin skin in her face, I could see the definite outline of a skull; a vague circular blueness around the hollowed eyes, the high points of the bone almost protruding out of the skin, her teeth yellowish and mottled ■. It was certainly different to the picture her mother showed me of Fay at 10 years, a happy, smiling child ■. She noticed my shocked face, and looked puzzled.

This was a young woman of 26 years, with the most supportive husband and caring parents. She had a steady job, and enjoyed a wide range of activities outside work. She was looking forward to having children of her own, and had only agreed to see her G.P. as her menstrual cycle had ceased.

He took one look at her then called the Registrar and the Hospital and a Social Worker. Fay was sectioned immediately➤. She was too weak to offer much resistance, but kept repeating that there was nothing wrong, only her periods■.

She hadn't minded, talking about herself and her feelings but the minute I mentioned her weight, casually, I noticed her thin hands gripping the chair ■.

On the Ward Fay was weighed every day. When meals arrived, one of the Mental Nurses would sit with her to make sure that she did not hide or vomit her food. When the Nurses weren't looking, the plants on the Ward and toilet cisterns received the squashed up food■. Mostly, the Nurses were wise to this deadly game.

It was weeks later before I finally managed to get through. It was after her friend on the Ward, Janine, had died. Janine was 22, and weighed 4½ stones■. Fay was very quiet, very subdued. She started talking about how sometimes people might see things that weren't quite right; not like hallucinations, just 'sort of narrowing things down a bit'.

We began to talk more after that≻; about magazines, and the 6 'Supermodels' ◆. We talked about getting older and she agreed that was scary◆. We never talked specifically about Fay's weight or Fay's food. We just came to an understanding.

One day, she just blurted out about the rape◆. After that, things between us just got easier. Sadly, she split up with her boyfriend soon after; they just could not cope with the emotional strain of it all. I finally discharged her, two years later. I remember her waving, walking down the drive. She was still elfin like, with the huge eyes of an African child.

Mania

Many of our finest creative people have and suffer from this illness, which is characterized by periods of intensive activity, rapid bursts of energy, irrational (or creative?) thinking and controlled hysteria. The moods are totally opposite to those of a depressive illness.

The illness can exist on its own, or coupled with depression, when it is called 'bi-polar' or manic depression. 'Bi-polar' refers to the extreme ends of the moods.

A manic attack cannot be controlled. The brain chemistry is firing off at a huge speed, and only medication can bring the sufferer 'down' off the high. In its early stages, it is akin to those occasional moments of extreme happiness we can all enjoy. Sometimes, a person with a manic illness can take back control, but the mood is heady and once that chemistry has started firing, then it is difficult to control.

Imagine wanting a quiet time, but your brain chemistry will not let you rest, just like the fairy tale of the girl in the magic dancing shoes. The body needs rest, but the brain will not allow it.

Mania as a Reaction to Depression

People who suffer depressive illness are prone to attacks of mania, when they come out of a low mood swing. It is a reaction which says 'that was hellish. I must be over happy to compensate.' And so, the mood becomes manic or 'high'.

Symptoms list:

Physical
❖ Increase in energy 'psychomotor agitation'
❖ Marked increase in activity levels
❖ Decreased need for sleep

Mental
❖ Patient has a highly inflated opinion of him/her self (grandiosity)
❖ Very talkative
❖ Lack of concentration
❖ May indulge in 'sprees' of sexual activity, buying or investing

❖ Fear at their 'out of control' situation, but unable to control it

Causes:
♦ Imbalance of brain chemistry
♦ Family history of the illness (genetic factors)
♦ Over reaction to recovering from a period of depression
   Abuse of alcohol or drugs

Cures/ Remedies
➢ Medications which change the brain chemistry
➢ Psychotherapy
➢ Behavioural Therapy

Look out for the corresponding bullets in the description of the illness ■ ♦ ➢

Case History - Mania

Esmerelda
"I'm just coming down now, over the last day or so. I try to enjoy the mood when comes on. There's usually no warning, just a buzzy feeling, like champagne bubbles in my blood. Things start to get better. Funny thing, even the grass is brighter and greenier■. I am aware of a tremendous, powerful burst of energy ■, and you know, I feel I can do anything!

I went shopping last time" (she points to her wardrobe, which is bursting at the seams with colourful clothing), "look at that lot! The credit card company was furious! It took months, and I'm still paying it all off■. I remember how it felt in that shop, and I was really enjoying myself. God, just like mother! ♦"

"And I keep picking up these men ■; you know, one night stands. It's really great at first, the sex, then I get uncomfortable, but it goes on.

144

And they are sometimes so scared that they leave, and I get mad and shout. I really want to sleep, but I can't and keep pacing up and down the room." She breaks off into loud sobs.

She breaks off, fetches a glass of water and a bottle of pills. "There. You see, I know I need them, but it's hard to remember. Lithium➤. Balances out◆➤the moods. Look at that." She holds out her hand; it is shaking visibly. "Been like that for years."

"It's like I've lived two lives, and not even enjoyed one of them. And I know they make fun of me; think I'm an old drama queen, and laugh behind my back. But honestly, Marianne➤, it they only knew what it was really like – I'm really scared inside■, and so exhausted. Oh, sometimes, I just wish I was normal, just for a while, to recover some energy." I, unable to say anything, just sit there and feel her exhaustion too■. I try to understand what her relatives must be suffering.

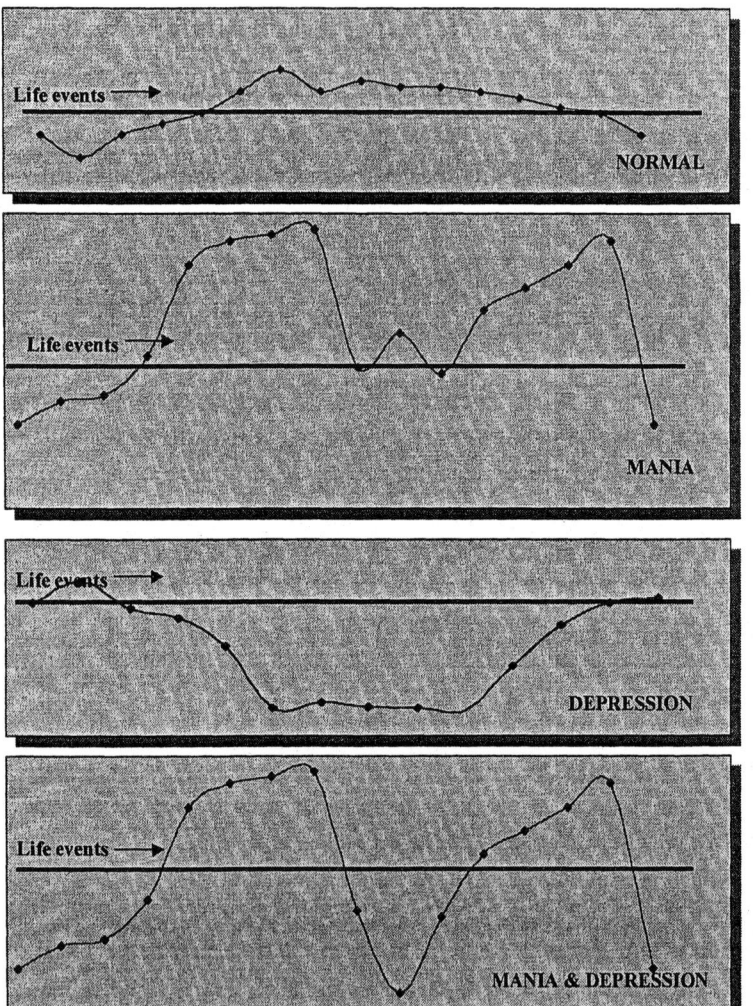

dotted line = progression of mood; up or down the 'base' line (black line)

Obsessive Compulsive Disorder (OCD)

We all might check doors are locked once or twice before going out, but when this "checking" gets out of order, then it becomes a crippling illness.

This is a very unusual disorder, with a huge variety of combinations and variations of symptoms, but whatever the actual cause and the type of 'rituals' undertaken by the sufferer, there are three common elements:

Obsession –   in Cynthia's case, this is her belief that everything in the house is contaminated.

Compulsion –   e.g. hand washing, which soon extends to compulsive body washing (we are not talking about what would be considered normal hygiene- this 'washing' can take several hours a day, and often is not stopped until the skin is broken and bleeding.

Ritual –   e.g. washing in a certain order, and use certain objects (e.g. fresh towels each time). If for any reason, the ritual goes wrong, it has to be completed from the beginning again.

Symptoms list

I have given one example of each type.

Mental – Obsessions
- Persistent ideas – e.g. their house is contaminated
- Persistent thoughts – burglars are going to raid their home
- Persistent images – crude sexual imagery

Physical – Compulsions

The 'compulsions' are repetitive actions, used to control the obsessive idea or image. These actions are sometimes called 'rituals'. The patient cannot control the ritual, which can take up the major part of his/her day. The numbered examples listed below refer to the respective numbered examples above.

- constant hand washing, (sometimes until the skin bleeds)
- repeated checking and testing of locks and doors
- constant praying to try to negate 'guilt' feelings

Causes:

- ◆ Imbalance in brain chemistry
- ◆ trauma, at any point in life

This can be long-standing or a short-term illness. The symptoms tend to relate to 'control'; obsessive people can be orderly to an excessive degree. It is not a common illness, occurring in 1.5 to 2% of people in a year.

Cures/ Remedies

➢ Cognitive-Behavioural therapy

Patients are given a 'programme' which is designed to very gradually reduce the amount of time spent doing the ritual. At the same time, the patient receives counselling to try to help him/her discover the original cause.

Look out for the corresponding bullets in the description of the illness
■ ◆ ➢

Case History – Obsessive Compulsive Disorder

Cynthia

Walking into Cynthia's home was like walking into a show home; nothing was out of place■. Her immaculate hair seemed lacquered into place, and every detail of her makeup was perfect ■. Nevertheless, as we spoke, I noticed her glancing regularly into a mirror on the opposite wall, brushing back imaginary strands of hair.

"I first started this.." she gestured helplessly with her hand, "this, well, cleaning ■, about a year ago. At first, I wasn't even aware of what I was doing. Marjorie, my daily help, eventually asked if I wanted to dispense with her services. I asked why, and she said that there didn't seem to be a need. I told her that the house was getting grubby, and I would need to give her an extra day."

Cynthia paused, then managed a smile. "Well, she was an honest woman. After a week or so of this, she asked to see me, sat me down on the sofa, and asked me to look around. I had spent literally all day, on my hands and knees, rubbing out every spot of dirt from the carpet, then at least an hour after scrubbing my hands. My hands were rubbed raw ■.

Cynthia sat for a while, looking at her hands, then looked at me with a wry smile. "Of course, it started soon after Geoff, my husband, died♦. He died of a chest infection you know."

She paused again, and I nodded. She gestured with her hands again, obviously unable to speak. "So" I said, "you wanted to scrub away the memories, as if it hadn't happened?"

"I feel it was more to do with blaming myself really. As if, the cleaning and stuff could somehow work a kind of magic and bring him back." She sat quietly thinking. After a few minutes, I interrupted.

"And now?"

"Now", she replied, "I can't control it. Honestly, I know what I am doing, but I literally can't help myself."

At that point, a large, red-faced woman opened the front door, and entered. Marjorie.

"Perhaps Marjorie can be a part of this programme. We will be doing something very different to your usual practice Marjorie. It will involve not cleaning➤, encouraging the dirt". Marjorie smiled and Cynthia laughed. I was sure from that point that this particular case was going to be a success.

Personality Disorders

The personality disorders are many in number, difficult to diagnose, difficult to treat and with no guarantee of cure. They range from the 'borderline', to full blown 'psychopaths', who literally have no 'conscience' (no one knows why). In many cases, there is a background of prolonged cruelty and abuse, stretching throughout childhood.

Knowing no other life, sufferers repeat the behaviour ingrained in them since childhood; the wife or husband batterers, the hysterical, the socially isolated, the murderous; unable to control the impulses which you or I, driven by goading, might just about resist.

Even as 'cases', they are hard to like, difficult sometimes impossible to treat. Even therapists, who are supposed to treat everyone in the same way, believe there must be improvement, have sinking hearts when dealing with this group of people. They are not likeable, pretty people.

Where do they go? What do they do for a living? The dirtiest of jobs, or the most dangerous. The jobs where human contact is not a daily feature. The ones you would not do. If their illness allows them to work at all.

Symptoms list:

These disorders are divided into various types, each with its particular characteristic.

The general feature are that the individual:
- behaves or reacts in a way markedly different from others
- experience problems over a wide range of behaviours
- the condition is of long standing

Physical
No marked physical symptoms.

Some Examples Of Types Of Personality Disorder
(with a brief outline of their characteristics)

- Anti social – shuns people and society
- Avoidant - inhibited
- Borderline – impulsive; difficulties in forming relationships
- Dependent – submissive and clinging
- Narcissistic – self obsessed
- Paranoid - distrustful
- Psychopathic – highly destructive form; unaware of their illness
- Schizoid – withdrawing and detached

Causes:

◆ Genetic factors
◆ Dysfunctional home life from early age

Cures/ Remedies

- ➢ Medications to control the symptoms
- ➢ Compulsory hospitalization ('Sectioning')
- ➢ Electro Convulsive therapy
- ➢ Psychotherapy
- ➢ Cognitive-Behavioural Therapy

Look out for the corresponding bullets in the description of the illness ■ ◆ ➢

Case History– Borderline Personality Disorder

Tom

"Never been married, myself. Since I was a child I have been alone. But if you told me that I would still be alone at 50■, in this grim little room I'd have topped myself long since. Thought about that a lot. Well, I've had many years of thinking haven't I? Lots of time alone to stew over."

He drags deep on a roll up, and blows the smoke at the ceiling, which is cracked, with a suggestion of brown ooze. An iron bedstead, covered in grubby bedding, sags in a corner. A cheap utility wardrobe and dressing table and two wooden chairs, the ones we are sitting on, are the only other furniture. A photocopy of Mung's "The Scream" is tacked with drawing pins onto the wall by the bed.

"I don't really know why you're here, but it's alright, as long as you don't stop too long. Can't stand company for that long. I expect they told you that, at the Hospital."

He drags again, and coughs. "What was it like? You mean working? Ah." "Couldn't settle at all, just one job after another; stores work, janitor, track worker, that sort of thing. Always some cocky bastard

152

and some boring louts, you know the characters well. I dunno". He seems genuinely puzzled, rubs his chin and stares at the floor.

"Week here, month there; whole year once! Wish I knew why. I just can't seem to get on with them, you know. Parents? Ah. Father was ex army, Corporal. Corporal Punishment I called him when I was a lad!" We share the joke, as he laughs and coughs at the same time.

"Yes. A great believer in the strap, a strong backhand to the face, and a fine stream of words he had for me◆. Friends? Na. No one was allowed at the house. Mother? Little timid woman, mousey. I didn't think much of her either."

"Love?" He laughs bitterly. For a second I think he is going to cry, but he controls it, and drags on the wet end of his roll-up.

"Oh, that stuff. He used to land her one regularly. Stop him? What for? That's what being married is about, ain't it■?. When I was older, used to land her one myself. That's how it is■."

"As a kid? I was never one for games and things, so I never joined in the playground stuff. Wanted too, but its hard you know. I used to watch how the other kids did it – sort of sidling up to the group, and then getting themselves into the game.

You know what kids are. Cruel little bastards. They seemed to sense something about me, and they'd all run off if I looked as if I was trying to creep up to them. He laughs harshly. "Well, I learned to bash them instead. I was known for it. Proud? I'll say ■, it was the only thing I had for myself, my fists. Dad would have been proud of me for that."

A tinge of regret in his voice. "Well, he died you see, so he never knew about it, my 'achievements'. Going? Now? But.. well you'll come again then sometime.." He coughs, shows me out.

As I walk down the drive, I can see he is watching me from the other side of the grubby nets. I know he will never admit it, but he dreads the years ahead of him, knows something is wrong, but it's too ingrained to do anything. Anyway, he would be too proud to allow any 'interference'. He may allow me back in next time, perhaps.

Phobias

Phobia's are genuinely felt but excessive "fears" about objects, things or situations. They can prevent the person living a normal life, if unchecked. It could be fear of going out, of an animal, of blood and needles, of flying. What they have in common, is that they start out very specific i.e. you are afraid of one thing, then that one thing encompasses the whole range of similar things.

The man in our Case History, was afraid of being in the cemetery, then this spread to his town, eventually, he was confined in his house.

Symptoms list:

To be classed as a Phobia, the condition must have lasted at least six months, which marks it from normal life anxieties.

Physical
No particular physical symptoms

Mental
- Excessive unreasonable fear of an object, thing, or place
- Avoidance of facing the fear
- Daily living is affected to a marked degree
- The fear is of long standing

Some Common Types Of Phobia
- Agora – fear of open spaces

- Arachna – fear of spiders
- Blood/infection – fear of being contaminated
- Claustro – fear of being in a confined space
- Obsessional Compulsive Disorder (see OCD)
- Post traumatic Stress Disorder (PTSD) – reaction after a major accident
- Situational – fear of a specific situation e.g. fear of flying, being in lifts
- Social – fear of social situations

Causes

- Excessive reaction to negative incidents in the past, connected with the phobia
- Worsening of an existing fear
- Reaction to a particular loss – e.g. loss of a loved one
- Reaction to an incident in the distant past

This condition is fairly common, occurring among about 10 – 11% of the population.

Phobias of all kinds are very common. We all have fears about certain things, but these fears are not considered to be 'phobias' until:

A   We start avoiding that object or thing regularly
B   The avoidance affects our day to day living

Avoiding a nuisance neighbour is not classed as a phobia! Causes are sometimes easy to discover, sometimes more deep rooted.

Cures/ Remedies

- Behavioural therapy
- Psychotherapy
- Cognitive-Behavioural therapy

This very common set of disorders is usually fairly easy to treat, using a behavioural therapy – the therapist will encourage the sufferer to face the situation they have been avoiding, but in a controlled way, and over several weeks or months. Look out for the corresponding bullets in the description of the illness ■ ◆ ➢

Case History - Phobia

Mike

"Its been getting worse in the last few weeks. Then, I could at least have got to the garden gate without the faintness ■. How long? I've been confined in the house for 8 months now."

He is neatly dressed, the house is bright and clean. The only thing you might notice is that he has moved his bed into the lounge, and it seems he is living in this one room. "If you'd told me a year ago that I would be afraid to walk outside my own front door, then I could never have believed it." He pauses.

"How? Well, it at Mary's funeral■. I got out of the car, and looked at the trees, I started to feel faint. The trees seemed to be coming in on me. Plenty of our friends turned up to say goodbye. After, we walked back to the cars, and I was feeling very dizzy. I was glad to get inside. After that, it was a succession of things■. At first, it was just going to town. We used to have a bite to eat in a café halfway, so I did the same, this time alone. After that, it got worse gradually■, until I had to shop locally. Eventually I could only get to the garden gate, before this wave of anxiety came over me. I'd tell myself it was ridiculous, but that made no difference. Each time I panicked, it was worse the next time■.

I thought if I stayed in the house, then it would wear off after a time. So, I found a home help to do the shopping and moved everything into this room, so I could avoid going out ■."

He looks really embarrassed, and with a voice tinged with anxiety, says: "Is there any hope that I'll get over this? I can't bear being confined ■. It's almost as if I'm in a coffin, like Mary." He bursts into tears and covers his face with his hands.

ONSET AND TREATMENT OF A PHOBIA

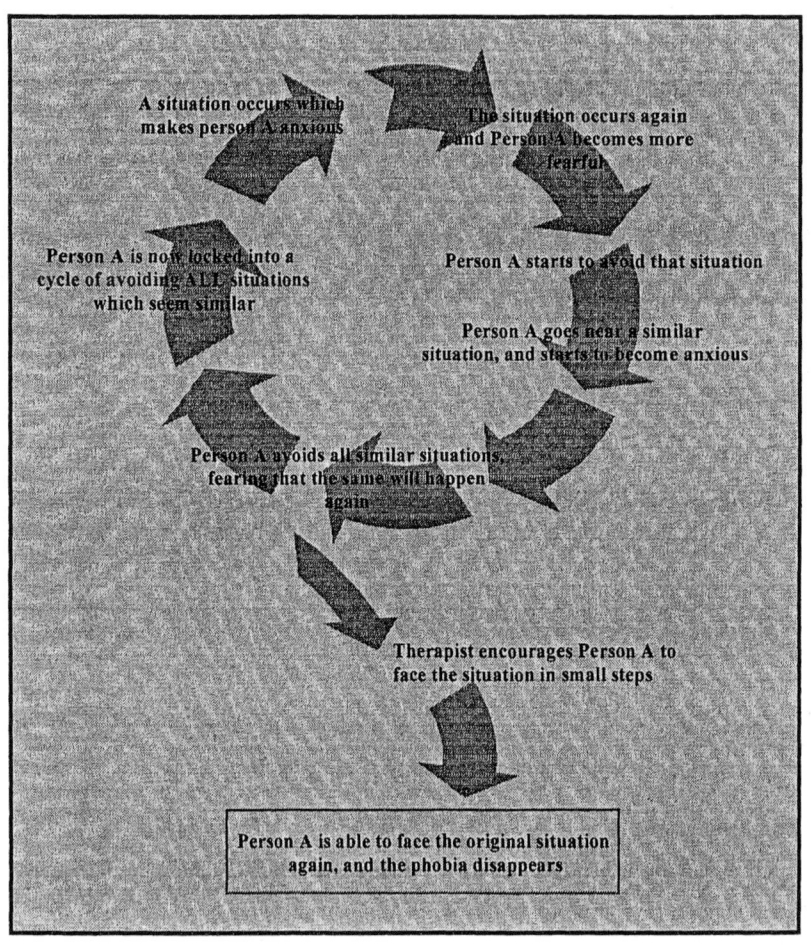

A situation occurs which makes person A anxious

The situation occurs again and Person A becomes more fearful

Person A is now locked into a cycle of avoiding ALL situations which seem similar

Person A starts to avoid that situation

Person A goes near a similar situation, and starts to become anxious

Person A avoids all similar situations, fearing that the same will happen again

Therapist encourages Person A to face the situation in small steps

Person A is able to face the original situation again, and the phobia disappears

Schizophrenia

Schizophrenia is a well-known but misunderstood illness. It is not split personality. A very few people are a danger to the public, often because they suffer frequent delusions of attack and are 'defending' themselves. Formerly, these people have been confined in a secure hospital.

This is one of the most severe mental illnesses for which there is no known cure. Medical people are not sure either of what causes it, although it is generally believed to be a combination of:
- ◆ Genetic factors – a family history of the illness
- ◆ A breakdown due to extreme stress

The effects of the illness are disturbing, with hallucinations and delusions in the form of visions and voices (refer to brief psychotic disorder, which has some of these same symptoms). Imagine what it must be like to have a nightmare, only the nightmare does not go away. Permanent and irreparable damage to the brain can occur. The hallucinations and voices are not all destructive or evil. They can be religious or benign images.

The treatment used to be lifetime incarceration in an Asylum. Now, medication can help reduce the effects of the illness so that some people are able to lead relatively normal lives, although for others that is impossible. Unable to cope, they start to wander. Sometimes, they commit crimes deliberately, because prisons a reassuringly regimented life, which appears to alleviate the chaotic symptoms of the illness.

Schizophrenia carries with it a huge stigma, probably the result of stories in the press of psychotic killers. These do exist, but are relatively few in number, compared with the number of people with this illness who daily carry out their lives in obscurity.

Symptoms list

The symptoms must be of at least 6 months standing. If you compare the symptoms with those of brief psychotic disorder, you will notice the similarities, although the former has a more specific cause and a far shorter term.

Confusion with Psychopathic Personality Disorder

Paranoid schizophrenia may be confused with "psychopathic" personality disorder. A Psychopath is born with no 'conscience' and therefore cannot distinguish between right and wrong acts.

Someone with schizophrenia is able to make such distinctions, but acts because he/she feels genuinely threatened, generally under the influence of powerful delusions.

Diagnosis and Cultural Factors

This illness needs careful diagnosis. Similar disturbances of vision and hearing can be drug induced. Some cultures are very tolerant of, and encourage some of the factors which in Western culture would lead to a diagnosis of hallucinations and delusions:

♦ Voodoo and witchcraft cultures
♦ Religious ecstasies, with spiritual images or 'speaking in tongues'
♦ Ancestor worship, where ancestors 'appear' and advise the living
♦ Spiritualists, who 'communicate' with the dead

The Psychiatrist has to take these factors into account when making this diagnosis.

Physical
▪ Sufferers may show general signs of a lack of personal self care
Mental
▪ Delusions; persistent and irrational thoughts or ideas e.g. of murderous attack

- Hallucinations; seeing or hearing things that are not there
- Speech can be meaningless ('word salad')*
- No feelings are apparent *
- Behaviour is disorganised or non-existent *

Types

Catatonic Schizophrenia
Now relatively rare, this type of schizophrenia has the effect of 'stupefying' the individual, who sits in an almost permanent comatose state. I remember one lady I saw, in the Asylum I worked in many years ago, who sat in the same chair for many years, taking her meals on her chair, and never speaking or moving. One of the student nurses made considerable efforts to talk to her, and the woman started to respond, only to sink back when this nurse left.

Paranoid Schizophrenia
A type of schizophrenia, where the person's delusions (false beliefs) are centred on one powerful delusion. This is the form of the illness which can be dangerous, particularly when the 'voices' are threatening and evil, suggesting to the sufferer that they kill. However evil and shocking the acts committed as a result, one has to remember, this is still an illness. Not everyone with this form of illness will murder, or even be likely to commit murder.

Causes

Generally attributed to one or more of the following:
- Family history of the illness
- Traumatic childhood/ family events

About 1% of the population is affected by one of these disorders, which generally begin during adolescence, although (more rarely) it can appear from middle age.

Cures/ Remedies

➢ Medications which change the brain chemistry
➢ Behavioural Therapy, in conjunction with medication
Look out for the corresponding bullets in the description of the illness ■ ◆ ➢

Case History - Schizophrenia

Mandy
Mandy is a bright, intelligent girl of 26, who has had schizophrenia since she was 15◆. She lives alone in a small flat, and receives irregular visits from her parents, and a weekly visit from her Rehabilitation Therapist.

After her breakdown, she had to leave her college course because she was unable to cope with the intellectual demands■. Her boyfriend left her when she was diagnosed.

"Of course I feel sad about not being able to work, only in a sheltered scheme, as the images are intrusive and sometimes the voices are so loud that I can't concentrate■. I set out to do Business Management and that grieves me too. I just want to be ordinary, but I know there is no cure. It took me years to accept that.

How did I realize something was wrong? I didn't notice; my parents did. I started shutting myself off from people■, it was difficult to concentrate. I kept feeling this fuzziness in my head, as if there was cotton-wool inside of my brain■.

Then, one day, I was on a boat on the Thames, looking over at the buildings on the other side. A rent appeared in the sky, as if it was a painting, and someone had ripped a great piece of it out, and there were bizarre figures in the rip■.

I couldn't make it out. I turned to tell my friend about it, and there was this horrible look of shock on her face. She couldn't see it ■ apparently or hear the voices. That really scared me.

After that, things started to get worse. I heard voices. I couldn't see their bodies, but they were very real. I couldn't bear the reactions I got when I told people, so I kept it to myself.

My College work was suffering; I had been working really hard for the examinations, perhaps far too hard◆. It was impossible to concentrate, with all these weird things going on around me. I knew I was getting insane, but was trying to ignore it, hoping it would all go away.

One day, I heard a voice■ saying that the boy next to me was going to kill me. I could see his face changing. He looked scared and then his face sort of started to melt. Apparently, I grabbed an art knife, and tried to stab him. That's when they called someone, and I was taken into hospital≻.

It was such a relief, to talk to someone. The Doctor seemed to understand, as if it were an everyday occurrence. I suppose it was, to him. Anyway, it made me feel better.

I asked him if I was mad, and he said, that madness was a term ignorant people used to describe something they couldn't understand. He said I had schizophrenia, one of the major mental illnesses, and that it could be controlled with the right medication.

I told him I was really scared; that I didn't mean to harm that boy, and that I didn't want to be locked away. I asked him if I would be put away, and he said that that wasn't necessary. As long as I took the medications≻he gave me, things would be fine, and that someone would visit me regularly≻ to make sure everything was OK.

I sort of got very lonely, especially as my parents rarely visit. I suppose its easier for them not to come. They couldn't cope with me at home, sitting around and talking to the voices. I believe that mum's sister had this too, so I suppose it brings it all back to her◆. Tom, the boy I tried to stab, still visits me. I feel really guilty, but he knows I believed the voices, and they haven't come back since I started taking my tablets.

He doesn't seem to find the fact that the flat is a bit messy; I can't get it together to clean up very often, as I get confused easily■. I kind of hope he visits more often.

Summary of Chapter

A useful exercise in diagnosis
Descriptions of:
- Brief Psychotic Disorder
- Depressive Illness
- Eating Disorders
- Mania
- Obsessive Compulsive Disorder
- Personality Disorders – some of the many types
- Phobias
- Schizophrenia

Each disorder described in the following pattern
- a brief description of the illness
- a list of symptoms
- causes, with an indication of recurrence in % of the population
- known cures or effective remedies
- A case history

If I asked you to enter a house, you might use a key, break a window, take the putty out of the glass, shin up a drainpipe. It depends upon circumstances; for instance, if there was a fire..

Marianne

Chapter 9

Non-Medical Approaches to Mental Illness

Contained in this chapter:
Social Interpretation
Harmony Of Mind, Body, and Spirit
'Stage of life' problems
Benefits of a balanced personality

There are many ways of looking at the whole question of mental health and mental illness. Sadly, some of the medical profession, particularly nursing, seem steeped in tradition. Those therapies which seem at all 'fringe' or less than academic are sometimes looked on with suspicion, even if they work for the patient.

Examples of therapies which at one time or another have been viewed in this way are;
- aromatherapy
- chiropractic
- osteopathy
- massage
- hypnotherapy

Massage for mental illness? Hypnotherapy for mental illness?

Let us leave aside the consideration that mental illness is about schizophrenia, paranoia etc. etc. It's about time, within this book at least, that we start to look at things in a different way. Mental illness is the opposite of mental health.

The only difference between a mild anxiety, which we all suffer from time to time, and a phobia is one of severity and treatment. They both are problems to do with the mental processes. I do not mean that that you are any more likely to suffer one than the other, but that, viewed in this way, mental illness becomes more 'acceptable' as being a variation of something we all, as human beings, undergo from time to time.

If someone is suffering a mild depressive disorder, or a phobia, there may be no need to go rushing off to the nearest psychiatrist for diagnosis. Something simpler may be just as effective. Only in cases of severe and intractable illnesses such as clinical depression or schizophrenia or one of the severe personality disorders require a psychiatric approach; but alleviation of some of the symptoms can be sought within the complementaries even for these. We all need basic human comfort and warmth, such as is brought by massage, or counselling, or aromatherapy.

There is plenty of room for all types of therapist, and those who would try to 'elbow out' therapies other than their own should surely look inside themselves for their motives.

I have used alternative therapists quite happily and quite effectively. I have also carried out therapy on myself. There is nothing more uplifting, than a pleasant aromatherapy massage, which gives the additional comfort of human contact, or a wonderful ¾ hour with a Jungian analyst. So, leaving aside tradition and fear, let us enter the 'complementary medicine' way of thinking.

Social Interpretation

There is a theory that there is no such thing as 'mental illness'; there is only a problem which exists between people who are not integrated within society properly. Given love, support, and understanding, then people will thrive.

They will also be tolerated whatever kind of behaviour they display; however, under these circumstances (the theory goes), then there will be little 'anti social' behaviour in any case.

We have only to look at the cultures of so-called 'primitive' tribes, where ancestors are revered. Attacks of what might in Western cultures be named 'psychoses', might be perceived by other cultures as being visits by ancestors who have inhabited the person's body. The person with such a psychosis will therefore be revered rather than reviled, and looked after within their own community.

This type of 'care in the community' of the real kind, rather than that artificially and unsuccessfully introduced in this country in the early 1990's, must surely be a positive pattern. However, it is very difficult to duplicate one culture onto another without also introducing the underlying belief systems which support the action.

Victor Frankl, a Jewish Doctor incarcerated in Auschwitz, said that a human being can survive terrible circumstances, and still survive both mentally and physically if there is just one circumstance – that he has a friend to share his feelings. If one can imagine the horrors of being in Auschwitz, knowing that a man can still walk out mentally whole surely this bears out the social theory.

Read also the many fascinating writings of R D Laing, a Psychiatrist who has some very interesting theories on 'the myth of mental illness'.

MAINTAINING PSYCHOLOGICAL BALANCE -
The Importance of Support Systems

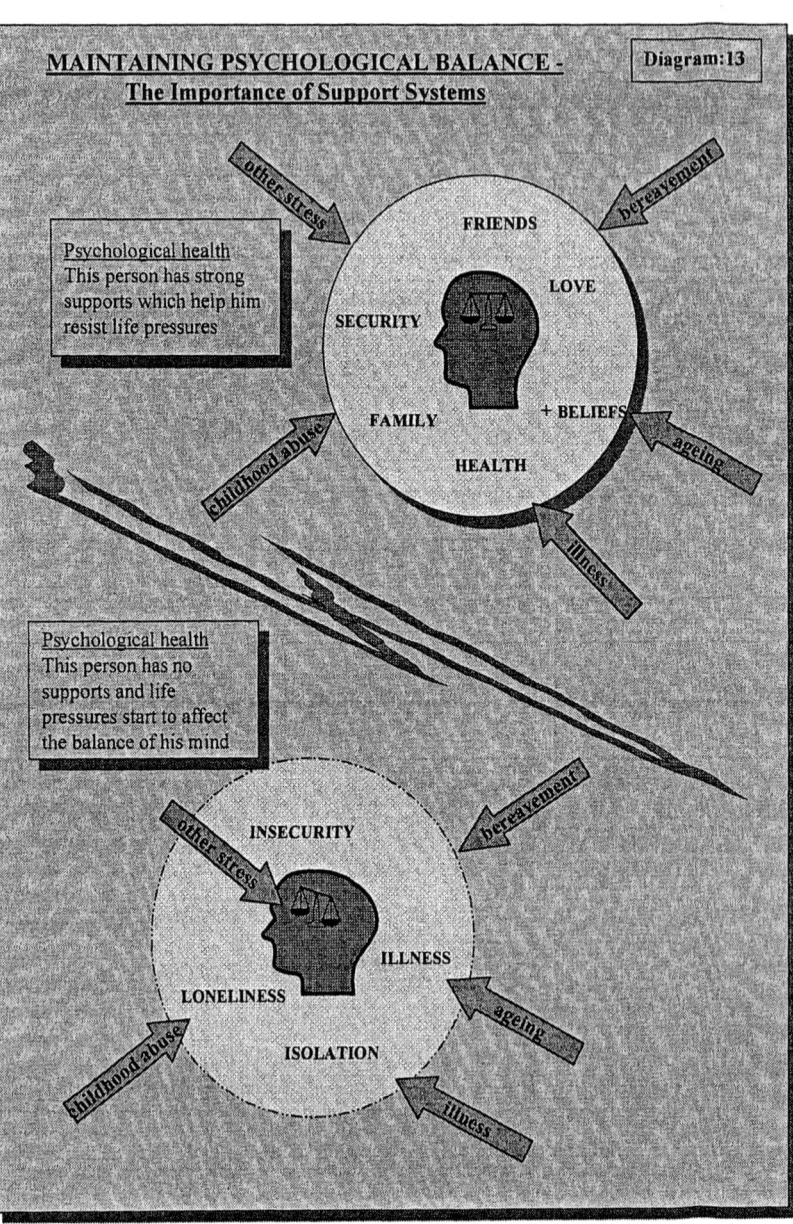

Psychological health
This person has strong supports which help him resist life pressures

other stress

bereavement

FRIENDS

LOVE

SECURITY

FAMILY

+ BELIEFS

HEALTH

ageing

childhood abuse

illness

Psychological health
This person has no supports and life pressures start to affect the balance of his mind

bereavement?

INSECURITY

other stress

ILLNESS

LONELINESS

ageing

childhood abuse

ISOLATION

illness

Harmony Of Mind, Body, and Spirit

Most prevalent among holistic therapists, and also those enlightened of the medical profession, is the belief that mental health and physical health (mind and body) affect each other. Treatment of one will therefore have a beneficial effect upon the other.

Imagine you have a cold; does it affect how you feel and think? If you are well, and the sun is shining, does that affect your mental state? There is a certain stability of mind, body, and spirit which harmonizes the whole person such that they will be able to live harmonious lives despite other considerations. There are many examples;

- Helen Keller – blind, deaf and dumb, a writer and teacher
- Anne Frank - Jewish girl who wrote her diary under appalling circumstances
- Richard Dadd - Victorian artist who spent his life in Bethlem
- Viktor Frankl – Auschwitz survivor, who became a famous Psychiatrist
- W.H. Davies - a tramp who became a celebrated poet & writer

I will give some details of the types of therapy practiced under the banner of 'holistic' medicine in the next chapter, but they are designed to work on the three levels of mind, body, and spirit.

The Benefits of a Balanced Personality

Within the harmony of mind, body, spirit, a person will be able to achieve far more in their lives. They will be at peace with themselves, and find themselves with energy to spare.

Refer to the diagram which follows. I have attempted to show the different areas as follows:

Mind –   relating to others, having suitable occupations, self identity, ability to relax

Body –   physical health and appearance expressing the best which can be achieved for that person, regardless of any physical disabilities, achieve sexual satisfaction

Spirit -   ability to perceive beauty, the arts, interest in matters spiritual, religious experience

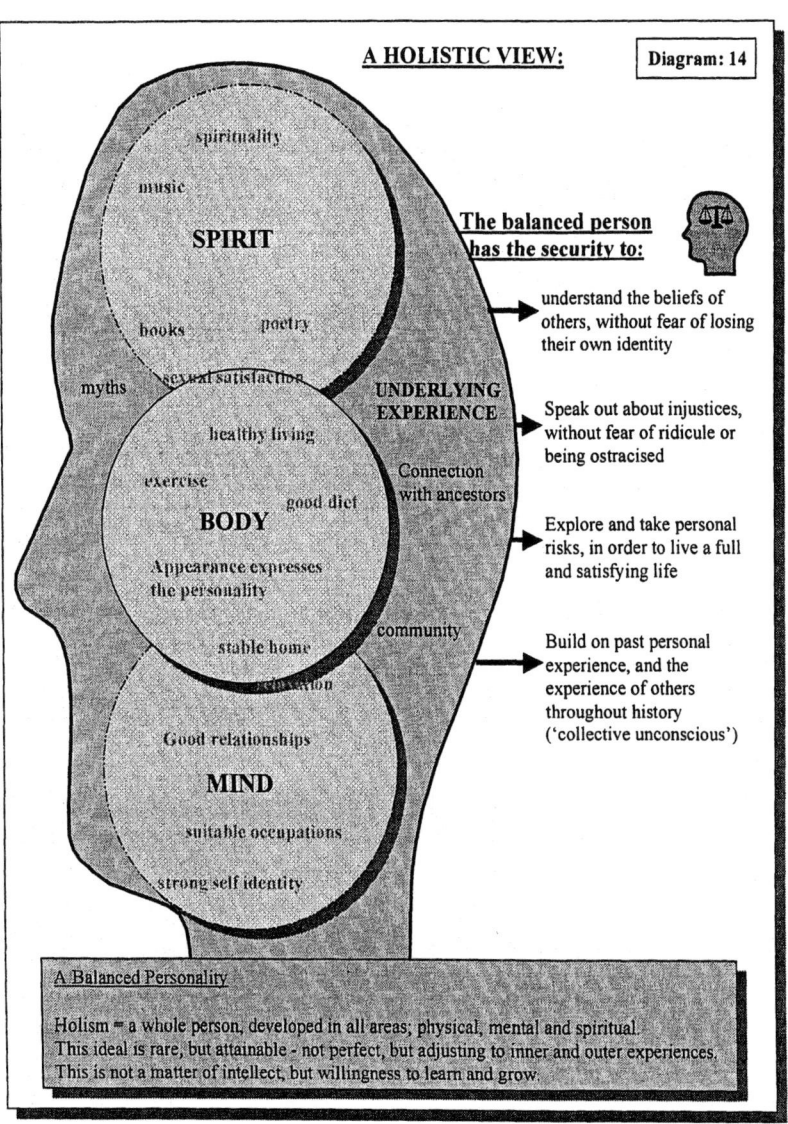

A HOLISTIC VIEW:

Diagram: 14

spirituality

music

SPIRIT

books   poetry

myths   sexual satisfaction

healthy living

exercise   good diet

BODY

Appearance expresses
the personality

stable home

education

Good relationships

MIND

suitable occupations

strong self identity

**UNDERLYING
EXPERIENCE**

Connection
with ancestors

community

**The balanced person
has the security to:**

→ understand the beliefs of
others, without fear of losing
their own identity

→ Speak out about injustices,
without fear of ridicule or
being ostracised

→ Explore and take personal
risks, in order to live a full
and satisfying life

→ Build on past personal
experience, and the
experience of others
throughout history
('collective unconscious')

A Balanced Personality

Holism = a whole person, developed in all areas; physical, mental and spiritual.
This ideal is rare, but attainable - not perfect, but adjusting to inner and outer experiences.
This is not a matter of intellect, but willingness to learn and grow.

'Stages Of Life' Problems

In all primitive cultures there exist 'rituals' or 'rites of passage'. At certain critical times in a human being's existence, there are important stages to be successfully encountered, with both physical and psychological factors. An example of how these stages could be described is:

- birth
- age 5 – going to school
- age 13 – puberty
- aged 18 – entering adulthood
- age 40's – mid life
- age 80's – old age
- ++ - advanced old age; facing death and whatever lies beyond

Rituals are marked with certain ceremonies, which are less likely in our society to be physical challenges, so much as involving dressing up in strange clothing, consuming food and alcohol, and receiving congratulatory cards.

We will all undergo these stages. Successful passage to the next stage depends on how well we have passed the stage before. I am sure we can all cite cases of 'puer eternis' (the 'eternal youth'), i.e. a man who never grows up; or the eternal spiteful person or gossip, who never learns to live at peace and lives to a lonely old age.

In cases where a 'mental' age block is reached, the Therapist will seek to assist that person progress from the stage where they are 'stuck' to the next stage. Jungians (followers of Carl Jung), are for example concerned with the important passage through the middle years. In the next chapter, I will describe some of the very pleasant 'holistic' therapies. My aim is to ask the reader not to close their eyes to new and unusual therapies; whatever works in a given circumstance is the best healer.

"A man may conquer a thousand warriors,
but the greatest of all is he who conquers himself"
Chinese saying

Chapter 10

Alternative or Complementary Therapies

This Chapter includes:
Complementary Practitioners
Aromatherapy/Massage
Art Therapies
Chiropractic & Osteopathy
Crystal Therapy
Reflexology
Spiritual pursuits
Yoga

COMPLEMENTARY PRACTITIONERS

So far, we looked at some of the many treatments for mental illness, based on the 'medical' model. The following are 'alternative', 'complementary' or 'holistic' therapies; the word depends upon your preference. These therapies work not only on the mind of the patient, but also on the body and the spirit. This theory is based on all three aspects, and one part cannot be treated in isolation. This theory is known as 'holism', as it attempts to deal with the whole person.

Many of the practitioners of the following therapies would make no claims for curing serious mental illness, but they are all very relaxing, which will promote stress relief, an important factor in maintaining mental health. This is why I am including them in this book.

There are many more therapies than I have room to explain in this brief chapter, including a very interesting 'Humour Therapy' clinic being set up in the USA by Dr Patch Adams, to which traditional medical people are flocking (see the movie 'Patch Adams' if you can).

Aromatherapy/Massage

Aromatherapy is a body massage, in which the Therapist uses beautifully scented natural oils, which are effective in treating specific disorders. Plants, as I am sure you realize, are also used to make the drugs and medications used in general medicine, and therefore come with a good pedigree. We in the West only recently discovered this; the Chinese have known it for thousands of years.

You might like to note that masseurs (male) and masseuse (female) are very good at strategically placing towels, so that their clients do not feel embarrassed at having their naked body exposed.

Once the body is relaxed, and the appropriate oils are working their way deeply into the body, the mind begins to relax.

This is an excellent therapy for people who do not like talking about their problems (particularly men). It provides the comfort of physical contact, without the added stress of feeling psychologically 'naked'.

Reflexology

This treatment has been known since Egyptian times, and is depicted on a famous tomb wall painting. The patient says "do not hurt me" and the practitioner replies "I shall act so that you will praise me"; the latter is depicted working on the toes of his patient. This practice has been used in China for thousands of years.

Reflexology is a gentle dry massage of the feet or hands, using talcum powder. It works on the principal that the body has meridian lines running through it in vertical lines, each line connecting areas of energy. When there is a blockage along one of the lines, which correspond to the soft organs the line runs through, then that will cause pain. The Reflexologist can find areas of blockage, and release them by massage, thus restoring the body to harmony.

These are the same meridian lines used by acupuncturists, the needles being pushed into the skin at specific points along the lines of energy. The meridian theory underlies much of the Chinese medicine system, working on the harmony or 'Tao' of the body and mind. Chinese medicine is a very interesting and worth researching if you are interested in holistic medicines.

Although Reflexologists are loathe to make claims about 'curing' illnesses of the mind, there is no doubt that this is a very relaxing and stress relieving therapy.

Art Therapies

Originally considered somewhat fringe, there are many people now taking to art therapies of all kinds. In art therapy, the patient will be given various mediums (crayon, paint, chalk) with which to draw. The idea will not be to create a technical masterpiece, but to allow the person to express emotions through the use of drawing and colour. When the piece is finished, the Therapist will discuss the meaning of the drawing with the patient. There are other types of art therapy, including poetry, reading, and psychodrama.

Psychodrama involves the patient acting out various incidents from their past, almost as if in a play. The various interpretations and different scenarios for the same sequence of emotional events can be explored in what can be very intense, but also enlightening, sessions.

The only real difference between art and art conducted as therapy, is that the latter involves psychological interpretation by a professional. Writing, drawing, and reading are in themselves excellent ways of de-stressing, whether or not they form part of an art therapy session.

Patients in Psychiatric Hospitals are always encouraged to take part in therapeutic activities such as these, whether they are conducted as formal art therapy or just relaxing pastimes.

Chiropractic/Osteopathy

Chiropractic is designed to restore health by manipulating the spine and joints by hand. The aim is to re-align joints which have become misplaced through bad posture, thus freeing any nerves which have become trapped in the process.

Often, when someone is undergoing stress or crisis situations, they will start to hold themselves differently; hunch, cringe, tighten up. Even in normal working conditions, with a large proportion of the population working daily with computers, posture will become bad through poor siting of the equipment being used. Even driving, with the stresses that brings, can seriously mis-align the body, and particularly the neck and spine.

Less gentle, but none the less as effective, is osteopathy. An osteopath will make sharper physical adjustments, which can be a little disconcerting to the beginner; the chiropractic which I received (with McTimoney practitioners) was certainly a much more gentle affair and just as effective.

Crystal Therapy

Natural minerals are very beautiful to look at, but this therapy proposes that the crystals themselves emit vibrations, which can be used to heal various aspects of illness; each type of crystal works on a particular wave length, and will therefore 'heal' a different problem.

Not a therapy I can particularly recommend from personal use, but on a pure pleasure principal, it is nice to own these lovely minerals, and to relax by looking at and feeling them. I have a theory that something of the giver of the crystal is retained, and that belief in itself makes holding such a crystal beneficial from the point of view of stress relief.

Beware, however, those who will try to sell you a crystal at a vastly inflated price, claiming that it has inherent 'healing' properties; buy them from a reputable mineral dealer and save your money.

Spiritual Pursuits

If you prefer approaching health from the spiritual side, try and find some books on Taoism or Buddhism. They are not the dry and complex tomes which you might expect, and have some very enlightening information on attaining peace of mind and body in simple and practical ways, by 'right thinking' and 'right acting'.

Try reading 'The Miracle of Mindfulness' by Thich Nhat Hanh (pronounced 'Titch Nat Han'), who advocates very simple daily practices to bring peace into your life, making even the most mundane of tasks enjoyable. Taoists are renowned for their peaceful demeanour and sense of humour, and certainly practice what they preach.

Yoga

For those who prefer something a little more physical, then try Yoga, which is the watered down Western version of the incredible exercises which the Yogis of India practice.

Yoga is a kind of exercise and meditation in one, and promotes physical and mental health, whilst also and most usefully promoting suppleness in the body. Yoga can be very physical, and consist of varyingly complex postures, which can be learned in easy stages. The postures are very ancient in original. There is also a less taxing form, which concentrates on breathing exercise; it is called 'hatha yoga'.

Yoga is now extensively practised within prisons, as a way of allowing both inmates and prison warders to relax and experience spiritual freedom, if not the real thing.

Chapter 11

Reading and Websites

Medical, Psychological and Analytical books explain why things happen; the arts give a vivid picture of the actuality of human life. You have only to refer to the drawings of Blake, the exquisite 'Faust' by Goethe, or the even the earthy poetry of patients from Bethlem Hospital to gain a real insight into mental illness. For these reasons, the reading list I have recommended is unusual for this type of book. It also contains poetry, fiction, and websites which portray the human condition in all its phases.

The web is a magical place. The sites range from the good, the bad, to the indifferent. If you really don't like meeting people, or are too shy, try surfing the Web for sites which appeal to your interests.

If you have read any books which you feel other readers might enjoy, or gain insight from, then do contact me via the Publisher, and I will add these in to any future edition.

And a small plea from me. Many years ago I had a book on the Teaching Tales of the Sufis, which is now out of print. If anyone has a copy, or remembers who the publisher is, please contact me via the Publisher of this book.

ART WITH MEANING

Psalms   *Unknown*
This is for non believers too. Pure poetic expression about the joys and sorrows of living
Selected Poetry   *Kathleen Raine*
A fine metaphysical poet – I love her work

179

Any paintings   *Blake*
An artist who successfully portrays madness, human suffering, and triumphs

The Plains of Heaven   *John Martin*
One of his religious paintings; sit by it and enjoy the depth of experience it expresses

Beyond Bedlam   *Publ: Anvil Press*
Poetry, written by the mentally ill. Very moving and worth reading for its insights

Free with Words   *Ed. Clive Hopwood (Writers in Prison Network)*
Experiences of the writers who work with prisoners, to enable self expression in all forms of the arts

BOOKS ABOUT LIFE IN GENERAL

Man's Search for Meaning   *Viktor Frankl*
Dr Frankl's own therapy 'logotherapy' explained, within the context of his own experiences during the Holocaust and beyond

The Road Less Travelled   *Scott Peck*
Self-improvement, by a very giving, generous man

The Prophet   *Khalil Gibran*
An understanding book about life, by a true poet

The Tao of Pooh
Learn to live, by re-discovering being a child

Jonathan Livingston Seagull   *Richard Bach*
A cracking story, about daring to be different

The House at Pooh Corner   *A A Milne*
A children's book, with many lessons for adults

The Door in the Wall   *H G ells*
This is about perceptions.

Be Still and Know   *Thich Nhat Hanh*
A Taoist monk who has some very practical tips for daily survival

When All You've Ever Wanted   Harold Kushner
Is not Enough
By the author of the best seller "When Bad Things Happen to Good People",
a Rabbi who teaches from the heart, that happiness lies in the small things of
life

The Diary of a Nobody   *G & W Grossmith*
A very funny book – Victorian – about all of us

BIOGRAPHIES/DIARIES

Daughter of the Queen of Sheba Jacki Lyden
Jacki's mother suffered severe mania, and almost destroyed the lives of her
family. Jacki survives to tell the moving story of their lives

The Diary of Anne Frank   *Anne Frank*
A heartrending diary – learn what a child is capable of writing, under
appalling conditions

Viktor Frankl Recollections   *Viktor Frankl*
A generous and moving autobiography about this great Psychiatrist and
Psychoanalyst, who was incarcerated in the infamous Auschwitz and
survived.

The Horse Whisperer   *Nicholas Evans*
Read it as "People Whisperer" too, and you'll learn lots

THERAPY AND PERSONAL DEVELOPMENT BOOKS

My voice Will Go With You Edited by Sidney Rosen

The Teaching Tales of Milton Erickson
The teaching tales of the great American Psychiatrist, Milton Erickson, who used a combination of hypnosis and metaphor to successfully treat all kinds of patients

Uncommon Therapy   *Jay Haley*
The techniques of the late, great Milton Erickson

Love's Executioner and Other   *Irvin Yalom*
Tales of Psychotherapy
Interesting cases from the couch of Irvin Yalom, psychotherapist

Welcome to My Country   *Lauren Slater*
More tales of psychotherapeutic encounters with mental illness

How to Survive   *Dr Margaret Reinhold*
In Spite of Your Parents
A practical self help book and an explanation of Dr Reinhold's theory and work

If You Meet the Buddha on   *Sheldon Kopp*
the road, Kill Him!
The bizarre title belies the content of this lovely book of a journey through the psychotherapy of Dr Kopp's patients – and himself

Creative Visualisation   *Shakti Gawain*
A favourite with 'New Age'ers everywhere, and a useful introduction to the art of visualisation as a life enhancing technique for everyone

The Silva Mind Technique   *José Silva*
Exercises to improve memory, concentration, and break free of those self limiting patterns of thinking

Games People Play   *Eric Berne*
Dr Berne sees through those irritating games many people play; and teaches you how to recognise and avoid them

Self Mastery   *Swami Paramananda*
A little book with a big heart, by an acknowledged master of Eastern spiritual traditions. A wonderful book for finding peace through traditional meditation practice and the training of the mental faculties

MEDICAL BOOKS

Dibs, in Search of Self   Virginia Axline
How a lost child was brought back into the world by a Psychotherapist

Touched with Fire   Dr Kay Redfield Jamison
02-916030-
Manic depressive illness – and creativity. A gem.

DSM IV*   *American Psychiatric Association*
0-89042-068-8
This is THE diagnostic manual, as used by the Medical Profession. Interesting to dip into, but heavy going for the lay-person.

Final Exit   *Dr Derek Humphry*
0-440-50785-5
This is the controversial 'suicide manual', written by a Medical Doctor, who helped his first wife end her life. She was suffering a terminal illness. The author does not persuade people to end their lives without some deep consideration, and talks about the effect on family and friends. He also makes suggestions about arrangements and 'goodbye' notes. I found this a highly humanitarian approach to an extremely sensitive and difficult subject.

Feeling Good, The New Mood Therapy   Dr David D Burns
Signet (USA)
If you can get hold of a copy of this (I believe it is out of print now – mine was from a second-hand bookshop), then do. Based on Cognitive Therapy, the book is practical and helpful. One of the best 'self-help' books I have ever read.

The Man Who Thought His Wife Was a Hat   *Dr Oliver Sachs*
This author, a Psychiatrist, gives excellent portrayals of some of the patients he met, who suffered aphasia – an illness which prevents them properly translating what they 'see'.   Well worth reading, not only for learning about the bizarre complications that brain damage can cause, but also for the very inventive ways the sufferer and their Therapists can find to overcome these situations.

The History of Bethlem   *J Andrews, J Briggs et al*
Routledge
This looks to be a good read, for those interested in the early treatment of the mentally ill. I certainly enjoyed the Bethlem collection of poetry.

INTERESTING WEBSITES

Site URL (address)   Site Content

http://www.mentalhealth.com
Mental health information

http://www.hyperguide.co.uk/mha/
Mental Health Act

http://www.rcpsych.ac.uk/
Royal College of Psychiatrists information on all aspects of mental illness

http://bookmag.com/books/nonfiction/168.html
Mental Health books

http://www.freud.org.uk/Index.html
Freud Museum

http://freudpage.com/en-us/freud/psychodefinition.html
Psychoanalysis - Freud
http://www.healthatoz.com/
A miscellany of interesting information on health topics, both mental and physical

http://www.ipa.org.uk/
International Psychoanalytical org

http://www.naswdc.org/PiecesNASW/adams.htm
Social work link in the USA

http://www.rgu.ac.uk/subj/pharmacy/pharmacy.htm
School of Pharmacy web site

http://www.hull.ac.uk/home/prospectus/undergrad/social_work.html
Training in Social Work

http://www.birchprojects.com/~kstrong/B006.html
"The Anxiety Disorders" Bookshop

http://www.openhart.demon.co.uk/idea/psychward.html
A personal story of a man with Hypomania

http://www.patient.org.uk/
A UK medical site on all aspects of mental and physical health

http://www.askyourpharmacist.co.uk/
Pharmacists and what they do – excellent!

http://www.nmhc.co.uk/
Drugs used for the control of mental illness

http://www.depressionalliance.org/
Mental health generally

GLOSSARY of TERMS

A

acupuncture	Chinese medical treatment, for re-balancing energy
agitation	*see* 'psychomotor'
agoraphobia	fear of open spaces
anaesthetic	drugs which render a patient unconscious or impervious to pain
analgesic	pain killing drug
ancestor worship	tribal culture of venerating their dead relatives
anorexia nervosa	eating disorder, in which a person restricts their intake of food
anti psychotic	a drug which reduces the symptoms of a psychosis
anti social	a personality disorder, characterised by difficulties in socialising
arachnaphobia	fear of spiders
archetype	a particular character trait in the personality (Jungian theory)
aromatherapy	a body massage with aromatic oils
asylum	'place of refuge'. Victorian institutes for housing the insance
autonomous nervous system	that part of the nervous system which functions automatically
avoidant	personality disorder, characterised by 'avoiding' situations

B

beck depression inventory	a scored rating chart, for indicating depth of a depressive illness
behavioural therapy	a psychological therapy, aimed at modifying behaviour
Bethlem Asylum	second oldest Hospital in England; a former Victorian Asylum
bi-polar	a mental illness; alternating episodes of depression and mania
'placebo' test	inert medication, given to some patients as part of drug trial tests
blood/infection phobia	fear of blood, or of being infected by dirt, needles etc
borderline	a mild personality disorder
brain chemistry	the chemicals of the brain, produced by 'chemical transmitters'
brief psychosis	a brief psychotic episode of hallucinations, delusions
brief psychotic disorder	as above
BPS	British Psychological Society for training UK Psychologists
Broadmoor	A Psychiatric Hospital for the criminally insane
bulimia nervosa	eating disorder, characterised by bouts of purging and vomiting

C

Carl Jung	founder of Analytical Psychology and modern psychotherapies
case history	details of patient's life, with a psychological and physical history
catatonia	mental state characterised by total inertia
catharsis	Greek for 'purging'; in psychology, 'letting go' of negative trait
CDPOM	drug which can only be dispensed on a handwritten prescription
'checking and testing'	part of compulsive disorder; excessive 'checking'
chemical transmitters	the way brain chemicals are distributed to all of the brain cells
Chiropractic	manipulation of the spine and joints; re-aligns skeletal system
Cinderella	Archetypal fictional character, representing innocence rewarded

claustrophobia	fear of confined spaces
Clinical Psychologist	A Psychologist who practices within a Hospital setting
cognitive-behavioural	recognition and changing of poor behaviour patterns
compulsion	an urge to carry out a certain act or ritual
contra indicative	reacts badly with other chemicals (applied to certain drugs)
counselling	one of the 'talking cures'
crimes of passion'	a crime which was committed during an intense emotion
Cruse	An organisation which provides free bereavement counselling

D

dead-end job	work with no prospect of further training or learning
delusion	ideas which are perceived as real, but are only in the imagination
dependent	personality disorder characterised by clinging to another person
depressive illness	mental illness, characterised by intense hopelessness and sadness
diagnosis	method of discovering the illness or problem from the facts given
Diagnostic & Statistics	Manual for diagnosing mental illness used by Psychiatrists
disembodied voices	voices which are heard, when no one is around.
drugs	medications. Also used as a colloquial term for illegal drugs
DSM	see ' Diagnostic and Statistics Manual'

E

eating disorders	illness characterised by restricting food intake by various means
ECT	Electro Convulsive Therapy, given to treat chronic depressions
EEG	electro-encephalograph
electro-encephalograph	reading on a printed tape or monitor of electrical brain activity
empathy	having an understanding of a personal situation
extrovert	outgoing, confident personality

F

Forensic Psychiatry	Psychiatric work with criminal mental illnesses e.g. paedophilia
'fragmenting' of the mind.	*see* psychosis

G

General Practitioners	a Medical Doctor who practices in a general medical setting
genetic factor	where cause is attributed to the inherited genes
giving an illness a name	diagnosing. Giving an illness a name is prior to finding the cure
grandiose ideas	delusional belief e.g. someone believes he is God or a prophet
group therapy	a therapy conducted with a Therapist and several patients
GSL	general sale list; drugs available for sale at a Pharmacy

H

hallucination	seeing people (or objects) who are not there
Herbalist	therapist who prescribes herbs instead of chemically made drugs

'high'	term used to describe exaggurated emotions, as in mania
histrionic	personality disorder characterised by exaggurated emotions
holistic	therapy which considers the mind and spirit, as well as the body
hostile environment	living in difficult conditions, e.g. housing, financial, social
Hypno-Psychotherapist	Therapist who practices brief therapy, using hypnosis

I

'imbalance of brain chemistry'	brain's chemicals are not properly distributed; leading to illness
insanity	state of mind where the mental processes are not functioning
insight	ability to understand the psychological situation
introvert	thinking, inward looking personality
isolation	being psychologically separated from other people

J

Jungian Analyst	an Analyst who is a follower of the Jungian school

L

leucotomy	Psychosurgery, involving cutting of the frontal lobe area of brain
'life event'	an event which is vivid enough to be remembered long afterward
'living sculpture'	street theatre, in which performers imitate statues
lobotomy	see 'leucotomy'
Lord Chancellor	Senior Judge in English Law

M

mania	mental illness, characterised by intense moods/ frantic behaviour
MAOI's	monoamine oxidase inhibitors; anti depressive medication
'media image'	a 'type' of person, which has been encouraged by media attention
medication	drugs given to cure or alleviate the symptoms of an illness
mental handicap	an incurable condition, with permanent damage to the brain
mental illness	illness of the mind, not 'physical illness. Can be reversible.
Milton Erickson	Psychiatrist who invented a therapy using hypnosis
MIMS	manual of drugs and their characteristics, used by GPs
molecule	smallest particle of a particular chemical
mood swings (rapid)	where a person's mood changes dramatically
muscle relaxant	drug given to relax the muscles, usually before surgery
mutagenicity	ability of a drug to affect the chemistry of organs in the body

N

narcissistic	personality disorder characterised by extreme self interest

O

obsession	unhealthy preoccupation
obsessional compulsive	mental illness, characterised by obsessions and compulsions

old lag'	one who commits petty crimes, in order to remain in prison
Osteopathy	therapy involving manipulation of spine *see also chiropractic*

P

panic attack	sudden fear, usually onsets without warning
paranoia	extreme psychological fear
paranoid schizophrenia	form of schizophrenia with an obsession e.g. pursuit by devils
Patch Adams, Dr	American Psychiatrist, who used humour therapy
pen portrait	or 'vignette' - a written description, which describes a person
persistent ideas	unwanted ideas which will not go away
persistent images	as above, but visual images
personality disorders	mental illness, characterised by problems of the personality
pharmaceutical	relating to the pharmaceutical or drugs industry
Pharmacist	otherwise termed a 'Chemist' or 'Druggist'; or 'Apothecary'
phobia	fear
physiotherapy	a physical therapy, involving massage and manipulation
POM	prescription only drugs
post traumatic stress disorder	stress which occurs after a traumatic event, e.g. an accident
'pow-wow'	Similar to 'palaver'; tribal meeting, to resolve social problems
Primary Care	refers to G.P.s and the various therapists within G.P. Practices
Psychiatric Hospital	hospital for the care of the mentally ill
Psychiatrist	Doctor, with an extra qualification in Psychiatric Medicine
psycho analysis	analytical therapy developed by Sigmund Freud;
Psycho Analyst	one who practices the above
psychodrama	therapy involving 'acting out' scenes from the patient's own life
psychology	science of the study of human behaviour
psychomotor agitation	state of frantic activity, as in manic episodes
psychopathic	personality disorder characterised by absence of a 'conscience'
psychosis	intense period of fear; the mind is unable to function normally
psychosurgery	brain surgery
Psychotherapy	talking cure; patient is encouraged to develop 'insights'

R

religious images	hallucinations of a religious kind e.g. of the Virgin Mary or God
remedy	cure or therapy; usually applied to holistic medicine
ritual	ceremony to mark the main life changes e.g. birth, middle age
Royal College of Psychiatrists	UK professional body of Psychiatrists

S

Samaritans	organisation, started by Chad Varah, to help suicidal people
'scapegoat'	sacrificed animal or person, who represents 'sins' of community
schizoid	personality disorder characterised by detachment from society
schizophrenia	fragmentation of the personality, with delusions, hallucinations

189

School of Thought	A particular method of training; taught by an individual school
'sectioned'	slang term; detained under the Mental Health Act
serotonin & noradrenaline	two of the chemical transmitters in the brain
social phobia	fear of social situations
solitary confinement	form of punishment in prison; person is detained in isolation
'speaking in tongues'	'babbling' like speech; accepted in some sects as 'voices of God'
Spiritualists	religious sect, with Mediums who 'talk with the dead'
'split personality'	markedly different personality characteristics in one person
stimulant	drug or remedy which revives or increases energy
stress	the forces which determine action
suicide	taking one's own life
supermodel	one of the few fashion models who are regularly in the media
symptom	a sign, usually of an illness

T

'talking cure'	therapies which use talking instead of drugs to effect a cure
tangible	real
The Mental Health Act	In the UK, the Act concerned with care of the mentally ill
'The Scream'	famous painting by Mung; agonised ghost-like face, screaming
therapist	one who cures by using a particular therapy
therapy	cure for physical or mental illness; not necessarily medical
'took the bull by the horns'	an expression meaning 'grasped the situation'
toxicity	level of toxin or poison
trauma	shock
trepanning	cutting of disc shaped piece out of skull; primitive surgery
tricyclic	type of antidepressant; chemical structure has 3 ('tri') rings
'trip'.	hallucination induced by illegal drugs or part of psychotic illness

V

vignette	portrait of, a brief description of
voodoo and witchcraft	ceremonies of a particular cult, e.g. as practiced in Haiti

W

warrant	a legal document, usually for arrest or entry to private dwelling
'word salad'	babbling, as in forms of schizophrenia

INDEX

Admission for assessment 24
Admission for treatment 25
Affective disorders 61
Alternative therapies 173
Amarylis belladonna 55
Analytical psychology 65
Anorexia Nervosa 139
Anti-depressant drugs 57
Animal testing 52 53
Anti-psychotic 57
Applications for section 24
Approved social worker 23 30
Arachnophobia 66
Aromatherapy 165
Art Therapy 175
Asylums 26
Autonomous nervous system 36

Becks depression inventory 138
Belladonna 55
Bereaved 14
Blind tests 52
Brain controller 36
Breathing problems 142
Brear (Joseph) 13
Bulimia nervosa 139

Care in the community (Act) 22 117
Catatonic schizophrenia 161
Categories of drugs for sale 54
Change in mood 34
Charcot (Jean) 63
Chemical imbalance 41
Chemical transmitters 42
Clinical psychology 97
Community mental health team 35

Complimentary practitioners 193
Consent to treatment 27 28
Contributory factors to mental illness 41
Counselling 67 72
Court of protection 28
Crisis teams 22
Crystal therapy 176
Curare 5

Delivery of ECT 46
Depressive illness 131
Designing drugs 47
Detection (to diagnosis) 33
Development of psychosis 128
Diagnostic manual 37
Digitalis 55
Discharge 26
Drugs 46
Drug therapies 46
DSS 28

Eating disorders 139
Electro convulsive therapy (ECT) 28 36 42
Electro – encephalographic machine (EEG) 43
Emergency admission 25
Empathy 70
Envallaria mavatis 55
Epileptic fits 60
Extroverts 65

Family History of mental illness 41
Frankl (Victor) 167
Free association 64
Freud 63
Frontal lobes 60

General practitioner 35 75
General stages of a drugs trial 51

Genetic factors 41
Glaxo Welcome 53
Grounds for sectioning 25
Groups of drug types 54

Harmony of mind, body and spirit 69
Holistic practitioners 42
Hormonal implants 27
Human rights 2
Humour therapy 173
Hypnosis 63
Hypnotherapists 109 165
Hysterical paralysis 63

Imbalanced brain chemistry 43
Individuation 65
Institutionalisation 24
International drug trials 53
Introverts 65

Jung (Carl) 63

Large scale testing of drugs 52
Leucotomy 61
Lobotomy 27

Management of financial affairs 28
Mania 142
Manic patients 29
Medicines Act 1968 55
Medical diagnosis 38
Medications 46 56
Mental Health Act 1983 6 15 19 79
Mental Health Act Commission 28 29
Mental Health Managers 26
Mental health rehabilitation workers 102
Mental Health Review Tribunal 23 27
Mental Health Trust Board 26

Mental illness 14 15 16
Multi-cultural commissions 28 29

New drug trials 47
Non-medical approaches to mental illness 165

Obsessive compulsive disorder 147
Occupational therapits 113
Osteopathy 165 176

Paranoid schizophrenia 161
Patch Adams 173
Patient 23
Personality disorder 150
Pharmacists 84
Phobias 154
Phineas Safge 60
Physiotherapy 36
Physical examination 38
Placebo tests 52
Power of attorney 28
Power to enter (private places) 30
Pre-frontal leucotomy 60
Process of a clinical trial on a new drug 48
Professionals 23
Psycho-hypnotherapy 109
Psychoanalysts 92
Psychiatrists 88
Psychology 66
Psychiatric hospital 84 119
Psychosurgery 27 59
Psychodrama 175
Psychotherapy 6 100

Qualified social worker 23

R.D.Laing 167
Reflexology 174

Reforming the Mental Health Act 21
Rehabilitation therapists 102
Removal of people from public places 30
Renewal of a section 26
Responsible Medical Officer 23
Rituals 172
Rites of passage 172
Royal road to the unconscious 64

Sanity 13
Schizophrenia 100 159
Sectioning 20 24
Sedatives groups 57
Self help groups 119
Social workers 106
Stages of life problems 172
Statistics 31
Stress 16
Suicidal urges 132

Talking cures 41 63
Testing on patients 52
The Samaritans 120
Therapeutic communities 122
Therapists 68
Toxicity 51
Trepanning 60
Tribunal 27
Trycyclics 57

Victorian asylums 116
Virtual drug trials 53
Volunteer testing 51

White paper 21
Withholding of correspondence 29

Yoga 17